LINK

Link is an exercise in abstraction, causality, and modeling. It is about discovering and making visible interdependencies in complex systems. The author distills what she has learned in pithy insights. It takes discipline. You won't regret reading this book.

— Vint Cerf, Internet Pioneer

Link is the missing link to our understanding of unintended consequences of many of our decisions and actions. This is a book for the ages, moving both technology (like AI) and human decision making to the next level. Must read.

— V R Ferose, SVP and Head of SAP Academy for Engineering

There is an explosion today in the impacts, risks, and opportunities of many decisions by private or governmental entities intended to impact future events. Link is about understanding these decisions and causal relationships. Societal transactions are accelerating: many more than ever are intangible, and there are substantial complexities created by newly discovered information as well as the resulting increase of global interdependencies. Surveillance capitalism, especially as enhanced by AI, is also a substantial risk today. Link is part of the solution: a crucial resource to understand causal chains, especially with the goal of avoiding unintended consequences of decisions involving data and technology.

— Bill Fenwick, Partner Emeritus, Fenwick & West LLP

LINK

How Decision Intelligence Connects Data, Actions, and Outcomes for a Better World

BY

LORIEN PRATT

United Kingdom – North America – Japan – India – Malaysia – China

Emerald Publishing Limited
Howard House, Wagon Lane, Bingley BD16 1WA, UK

First edition 2019

Reprints and permissions service
Contact: permissions@emeraldinsight.com

British Library Cataloguing in Publication Data
A catalogue record for this book is available from the British Library

ISBN: 978-1-78769-654-9 (Print)
ISBN: 978-1-78769-653-2 (Online)
ISBN: 978-1-78769-655-6 (Epub)

Printed by CPI Group (UK) Ltd, Croydon CR0 4YY

ISOQAR certified
Management System,
awarded to Emerald
for adherence to
Environmental
standard
ISO 14001:2004.

Certificate Number 1985
ISO 14001

INVESTOR IN PEOPLE

For the future, Cymbre and Griffin Smith

CONTENTS

FOREWORD

Imagine a future a hundred years from now in which the human race has grown up. In this future, the major strategic decisions made by states and companies are almost always effective, because people understand how decisions *work*. Systems thinking has become ubiquitous.

In this world, many of our environmental problems have been solved, because we understand that the costs of mistreating it outweigh any short-term gains. Businesses operate ethically, because failing to do so reduces employee productivity and lowers profits in the long run. Wealth inequality runs at a tiny fraction of its former levels, because leaders across the world have learned the benefits of pressing wealth back into public hands. They have gained the knowledge and tools to better achieve their social goals by empowering and motivating a prosperous workforce. The result is a more stable, more equitable, and happier planet.

The book you're reading now is like a gift from that future dropped into the present. What Lorien has done here – and it is no small feat – is synthesize some of the sharpest current thinking from decision intelligence, AI, causal analysis, and behavioral economics into a decision making methodology anyone can use. The result is a deceptively simple system capable of enabling teams to reliably reach outcomes that are effective, robust, and intellectually honest. She has done this even while some of the research she leverages is still finding its way across the cutting edge of science.

I know this to be true because I've explored that edge. In the course of my career I've worked in around eight different scientific disciplines, as well as operating as a software consultant, entrepreneur, and author – writing the science fiction novels for which I'm most well-known. I've seen what is and isn't there yet in fields as diverse as machine learning, evolutionary biology, and behavioral psychology. With that perspective, Lorien's work leaves me both delighted and impressed. In fact, my first thought on reading her book was "dammit, why didn't I think of doing this?" But therein lies its genius.

I felt deeply honored when she reached out to me, and on reflection believe that she wanted her foreword to reflect the voice of someone who'd see the scope of what she'd achieved. When you develop an idea that's immediately accessible, it's easy for some to miss the hard work it took to formulate, by virtue of its very ease of adoption. However, I recognize the books and research papers Lorien touched to make *Link* possible. I can easily infer the sheer amount of invested time working on real-world problems that must have been required to refine the method. As a result, my hat is permanently doffed in respect in her direction.

Lorien makes strategic decision making look easy. But don't be deceived. It's not. (Or at least, not unless you have a copy of *Link* in your hands.) Otherwise, we'd already been living in that golden future I described. In fact, making good collective decisions is getting harder. As the pace of change accelerates, and the social variables multiply, making the right choices is more difficult than ever. And my own research strongly suggests we should expect that trend to worsen before it improves.

One reason for this is that as the world becomes more interconnected, the number of feedback effects between populations, industries, and the environment increases non-linearly. This means that the timescale at which we can anticipate world events is shrinking fast. And with eight billion people in the world now making ten thousand interrelated but uncoordinated choices every day, global volatility is skyrocketing.

Furthermore, the technology we've built to help us navigate this complex modern world can only help us so much. Data science and AI can only work when regular patterns exist in data to be found. They are far less effective when presented with the output of a rapidly evolving chaotic system. The right tools to manage such a world will be those that capitalize on data, but yield control to the best learning systems we know of for handling complex, multi-level stimuli: human teams. They will be the tools that clarify how every one of us can make better choices each day that bend the arc of the future toward hope.

What this means is that techniques that empower us to find rational, cooperative outcomes to the world's problems are more important now than at any prior time in human history. In fact, the only way for us to get to that golden future is to pick up tools like the one Lorien has laid before us and make active, vigorous use of them as quickly as possible. It's my deepest hope that the method in this book sees broad adoption and sets us firmly on a path toward a reality we can all be proud of.

Alex Lamb

INTRODUCTION

*The way that you think about the future directly impacts the
actions that you take today. However, our Industrial Age models
have driven short-term horizons in business, government and
society, and this has caused us to think and act incrementally, in
silos and linearly. Fundamentally, this is a limited and antiquated
approach, and will not lead us to the future we want.*
— Frank Spencer and Yvette Montero Salvatico
(Kedge/The Futures School [1])

Why aren't the most powerful new technologies being used to solve the most
important, "wicked" problems: hunger, poverty, inequality, conflict,
unemployment, disease? What's missing?

Solutions to these kinds of problems require new ways of thinking, and
new ways for people to work hand-in-hand with each other, and with
technology, to take actions that go beyond just predicting the future, to
understanding how to change it.

Think about it: virtually all daily human activities are directed toward
some future outcome. Yet our historical ways of thinking about how our
actions lead to outcomes have been limited.

This should come as no surprise given the historical constraints on
resources, like life expectancy, communications, and availability of
information. For our primate ancestors, these limitations meant that
planning ahead was not much of an option. The future was something to be
survived, and little else.

Civilization — which ultimately brought about written records and more
rapid dissemination of information — empowered us to seek competitive
advantage by predicting our future. We needed to understand the seasons,

1

anticipate conflict, and track relationships within a community. Cognitive capacity was still a limitation, though, as was the availability of data. These constraints were pushed to their limits.

Today, we are in a qualitatively new era, where the information and analysis resources available to us to understand the future are, for all practical purposes, "boundaryless." Terabytes of data surround us, waiting to be understood. Artificial Intelligence (AI) stands hand-in-hand with more traditional disciplines like economics and statistics to shed light on the most complex situations. And our ability to communicate and collaborate using modern technology is practically unlimited. What will our relationship with the future be in this new boundaryless world?

I believe that our role now is to *responsibly create our future*. We have always had the power to *change* our future. This is completely different. The changes we orchestrate will be intentional, global, and focused on long-term and distant impacts that were previously impossible to understand.

Without stepping up to this responsibility, unintended consequences will inevitably multiply.

To fulfill this new role in our relationship with the future, major shifts in perspective are not only possible, but essential. Contrary to many forecasts, as you'll learn in this book, we are not about to become slaves to Big Data and Artificial General Intelligence (AGI) robots. "Today's future" will rely more heavily on human vision and imagination than ever before. We are injecting greater purpose and diversity into our thinking, which must reach many generations into the future. Distances between cause and effect will shrink to insignificance. We must embrace complexity. And our feelings about the future are more important than ever.

Because perspectives have been slow to shift, we haven't yet adapted well to this third era of human existence. Many feel overwhelmed with information, freezing them into inaction. Most struggle to see the impacts of their actions on the world at large. A child in Syria is in danger, what can I do about it? I hear the ice caps are melting, I feel helpless to make a difference. Without a clear picture of how the actions we take impact events at a distance, it's hard to take the right step.

This book is about an emerging movement, embraced by dozens of companies and thousands of people worldwide. This movement seeks to link action today with visions of a better future. The way forward is emerging from disparate threads that are only beginning to be woven together.

Barriers between disciplines are starting to dissolve, and we are weaving together technology, mathematics, history, philosophy, the social sciences, spirituality, geological and biological sciences, governments, and the earth itself.

Certain themes infuse this movement. "Democratization" – making things easier to use for everyone without removing their power – is a core principle. Very sophisticated cars can be easy to drive. And just because fields like economics, AI, and machine learning sound daunting, doesn't meant that we can't build a "driver's console" that can be operated by mere mortals. Computers were pretty intimidating to everyone a few decades back, yet today they're everywhere. The same change will happen with many of today's technologies.

Another core theme of this book is to move back to integrating humans with technology. Hollywood (and some thought leaders, but not most AI experts) would have us believe that a takeover by AGIs – some of which are terrifying robots – is just on the horizon. These stories distract us from the truth, however, which is that the next great leap forward in AI is about bringing humans back into the loop. The reason why – as I'll be explaining throughout this book – is that humans understand how the systems of the world operate, its cause-and-effect structure, in a way that computers don't, and won't be able to learn for a long time.

This book is about getting serious about the purpose that the systems we build will achieve, and working together to understand how to make decisions, which lead to actions, which lead to outcomes. It invites connection between head-in-the-clouds and feet-on-the-ground actions. Even the most sophisticated computer program must be written with a purpose and a value system, and this requires a human touch.

So in this boundaryless third era of human evolution, we can shape our future as never before. Diving into this world you'll learn about fascinating and powerful breakthroughs like deep learning, multi-link thinking, warm data, intelligence augmentation, transfer learning, and the re-emergence of cybernetics. You'll learn how to leverage "known knowns" and to search for both "known unknowns" and "unknown unknowns" to enter a new mode of thinking.

You'll also learn about how humans are shifting, from auditory/text analysis of hard problems to the visual/spatial/kinetic. You'll learn how to combine creative thinking – about your dreams and actions available to you – with concrete steps that you can take tomorrow. You'll learn about how organizations worldwide are using these techniques to solve previously impossible problems, and how you can learn from them to think more clearly about your own day-to-day life.

And you'll understand why and how all of these new concepts converge around *decisions*, which are how both humans and computers connect actions to outcomes, and why this movement is being called Decision Intelligence (DI), which is being used in many arenas, from employment disability inclusion [2], to government budgeting [3], customer care, enterprise risk management, capital planning, and much more.

A number of companies identify themselves with the "Decision Intelligence" name, including Gongos, Busigence, eHealthAnalytics, Satavia, Powernoodle, TransVoyant, TransparentChoice, Puretech, Element Data, Gilling.com, Mastercard's DI initiative [4], and Quantellia. Others are focusing on DI (sometimes called "decision engineering") as a core capability, including Google, infoHarvest, Lumina Decision Systems, Prowler, van Gelder and Monk, and Absolutdata. Several companies claim to – or are rumored to – include DI groups internally, including Groupon, Urbint, Grubhub, Microsoft, AIG, DNV GL, Fair Isaac, and Uber. Alibaba – the world's largest retailer – also runs a DI research laboratory [5].

By reading this book, you'll learn from the leaders of this movement to improve decisions in your own life and work. The rewards will be immeasurable whether you're a retiree, politician, or a Fortune 100 executive, a high-school student, or an academic researcher.

And, if you're a technologist interested in AI and Big Data, you'll learn about where you fit in the DI ecosystem, and about how DI is, for many, the next step in the evolution of AI.

The boundaryless future is both fascinating and fun, so hold on to your hats. Let's take a ride!

CHAPTER 1

GETTING SERIOUS ABOUT DECISIONS

What's the best way to begin to link technology and data with humans in this new world? Doing so can seem overwhelming, unbounded, and it's hard to know where to start. Fortunately, a consensus is emerging worldwide that:

> **Key Insight #1:** A *decision* — the thought process that leads to actions, which lead in turn to outcomes — is the right "building block" for solving many of the world's most complex problems and for integrating humans with technology.

Why is this so? Everything you create or do happens twice: once when you visualize it and the second when you bring it into reality. And, when we visualize how our actions will lead to future outcomes, that visualization results in a decision.

This book is about how to think about decisions in a new way, which is connected to ancient patterns of thought, and is informed by unlimited sources of new information a greater ability to work together. The field is called decision intelligence (DI).

As I'll describe in more detail later on, NASA uses DI to decide how to deflect an incoming asteroid [6]; Google's chief decision officer Cassie Kozyrkov has trained thousands of engineers in DI [7]; DI is extending how AI is applied in the legal profession [8], and DI ecosystem members include enterprise tech giant SAP a greater smaller companies like Element Data [9] and Prowler [10].

SHIFTS IN PERSPECTIVE

To do this, you'll need a shift in perspective: technology alone solves only a small subset of the important problems. It must work hand in hand with humans who in turn work in new collaborative settings, which integrate the academic disciplines with nonspecialists like you (because everyone is a non-specialist in most areas) with technology, and with your friends – on social media and in person – who want to go beyond conversation.

This change in thought demands, in turn, a *problem*-focused position. Technology can be exciting, but it must come second; indeed, it can create huge distractions. For example, we may become so enamored with "smart" city sensor technology that we lose sight of the fact that simply improving human collaboration would lead to a better solution to the issues we face. By starting with problems and desired outcomes and then working backward to actions by way of data, artificial intelligence, human expertise, complex systems analysis, economic theory, and more, we obtain a greater focus, and problems become solvable in new ways.

Much as early telescopes were an important part of the shift in our understanding of the heavens, the focus that we obtain by tracing back from the outcomes we wish to achieve to the actions we take to achieve those outcomes, and then to the decision making thought process, drives a powerful change in a world that is otherwise looking for a technological "silver bullet."

Another shift in thinking is from breaking problems into small parts – called *reductionism* or *analysis* – to understanding how those parts work together – called *synthesis*. Reflecting this movement, for example, an early pioneer is intelligence expert Josh Kerbel, who calls himself an "intelligence synthesist" instead of the more familiar term "intelligence analyst" [11].

You'll also need to go beyond verbal and text-based thinking, to use the spatial and motor parts of your brain, which are older and, in many ways, smarter. In doing so, we're integrating technologies not only with each other, but also with the management and social sciences in a powerful new way.

THE DI SOLUTIONS RENAISSANCE

The only way that we will be able to successfully address our grand challenges is through the practice of meshing. In our age of exponential complexity, one plus one does not always equal two. When we intentionally combine the various elements of art and science, we will discover new ideas and solutions. We have not solved some of our biggest problems because we have siloed our disciplines, and this granular approach has actually caused those problems to be exacerbated. The sweet spot of discovery is in the middle - the relationships between the disciplines [...].

— Frank Spencer/Yvette Montero Salvatico
(Kedge/The Futures School [1])

The potential of DI cannot be overstated.

DI does not replace existing technologies. Indeed, it supercharges them by unifying them into a single framework. It also bridges them into a form that is familiar and natural to non-technical decision makers.

In addition, DI is today becoming a unifying framework within which a "solutions renaissance" is also emerging, promising to solve some of the most important problems we face, like poverty, climate, conflict, and more, as shown below in Figure 1.

The left-hand side of Figure 1 shows several disciplines that have histori-cally been explored separately: a game theorist may understand some AI, but not enough to use it effectively; an expert in Big Data may have never even heard of Operations Research. The challenge we face today is illustrated by

Figure 1. A Solutions Renaissance, Driven by Decision Intelligence.

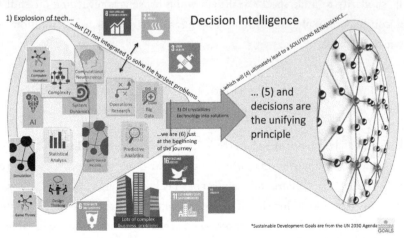

Figure 2. WorldSummit's View of the Upcoming Human Phase Shift.

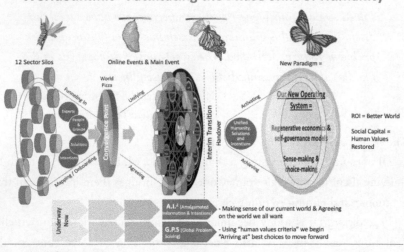

Source: WorldSummit.global.

the arrow in the center of Figure 1: to develop frameworks and other "glue" techniques to get these disciplines working together to solve the most important problems. And the overwhelming evidence is that decisions should be the focus.

But don't take my word for it. Check out the very similar diagram produced by the team at http://www.worldsummit.global/phase-shift/ (Figure 2). Its similarity to mine speaks to the emerging consensus regarding the shift to a consolidation phase which is creating a new platform for solutions to wicked problems.

Separating "Under the Hood" from "the Driver's Seat" Allows Sophisticated Disciplines to be Unified

Unfortunately, one of the characteristics of specialist disciplines is that they accumulate jargon over time, which can appear daunting for a "neo-generalist" trying to support this endeavor [12]. Although jargon serves a purpose — it allows for shorthand communication by specialists — it interferes with the most important task today, which is to integrate the disciplines to solve wicked problems. Given that it's impossible in one lifetime to learn the sophisticated language of so many individual fields, how can this be possible?

Fortunately, there's a well-understood answer that comes from engineering disciplines: to focus on the "outside of the box" instead of the inside. As pointed out by Google Cloud Chief Decision Scientist (and DI evangelist) Cassie Kozyrkov: "We don't have to be refrigeration experts nor microwave electronics experts to cook a good meal: instead we can interact with these kitchen appliances through easy-to-use interfaces [15]." And to enjoy eating the meal in a restaurant, we don't need to know a thing about the "back of the house": the kitchen and cooks who work there. Like Russian dolls, these complex systems are organized into layers. The connection between the layers is called an *interface*, the most well-known example of which is a user interface for a piece of software. Just as you don't need to understand your iPad operating system or how to write software to enjoy Words with Friends, it turns out you don't need to have a deep technical understanding to use an economic or artificial intelligence model.

The bottom line: don't let the sophistication of your Ferrari stop you from driving it, and don't let the jargon often used within AI or complex system dynamics stop you from making use of these technologies. The purpose of Chapter 3 is to build this bridge for you: to help you to understand these technologies so you can be part of the global movement to solve the wicked problems, if you like, or just those within your own life or organization.

An important side note: as a computer scientist and AI practitioner, I have a lot to say about AI, machine learning (ML), and software solutions. But don't be misled: my greater focus on technology compared to, say, economics, is merely an artifact of my own expertise and experience. Please don't take away from this emphasis that software is the most important element of the full DI discipline. It's not.

The Solutions Renaissance in Context

The Copernican revolution was based on a shift from the Earth as the center of the Universe to the Sun as the center of the solar system. This simplified very complex equations for planetary motion and also formed the basis for centuries of understanding of our Universe [13]. As described by Kuhn, the Copernican revolution also represents a pattern for paradigm shifts: changes in perspective that bring about great benefits.

Shifting to a decision-centric perspective and using the decision as the basis for unifying multiple fields of study has the potential for as great an impact as Copernicus.

Complex adaptive systems, whether single-celled organisms, bacteria, or the Internet, undergo what might be called a "breathe out/breathe in" alternation: an explosion of programming languages is followed by consolidation into one or two ... a period of great human exploration and creativity is followed by a consolidation into a few types of economy.

This rhythm of complex adaptive systems goes back millions of years (Howard Bloom calls the phases Diversity Generation/Conformity Enforcement [14]). The DI renaissance shown in Figure 1 fits this age-old pattern: an exciting journey for those bravely optimistic enough to believe in a bright future, driven by a phase shift in human potential.

Like other paradigm shifts, DI sheds light on complexity, providing insights and solutions that were not previously possible. Core to my approach to DI is a diagram I call the causal decision diagram (CDD). As I'll describe in more detail below, the CDD is made up of just a few simple parts. Like DNA, these parts can be combined to find solutions of great sophistication.

HOW DID WE GET HERE: THE TECHNOLOGY HYPE FEEDBACK LOOP

To understand how to untangle ourselves from current circumstances, it's important to understand some of the patterns that got us here. One is a technology hype feedback loop: the press looks for exciting stories, and technology *solution* vendors are much easier to reach for an interview than people with *problems* for the technology to solve. This leads to a lopsided media focus: we write about exciting technology, which then feeds back to technology companies, who use the press coverage to raise funds and plan strategically, which in turn leads to more availability for those press interviews.

This loop is exacerbated by the Internet and, despite the benefits of democratization of information, there are now massively powerful vectors of misinformation about topics like Big Data, Artificial Intelligence, Augmented Reality, Autonomous Vehicles, and more. But, says Google's Chief Decision Scientist Cassie Kozyrkov, the Internet also:

*expands access to information and allows people to peer over the
silo walls that used to separate academic fields, creating an
environment in which the interdisciplinary nature of Decision
Intelligence can thrive [15].*

THE CORE QUESTION

*Amid all the complexity, visual archetypes help us connect globally
with people on a basic human level.*
>   − Eileen Clegg, the founder of Visual Insight,
>   and the author of *Master Symbols* [16]

The core question of *Link* (and for most organizations and people working
in DI) is this:

*If I make this decision, which leads to this action, in these
circumstances, today, what will be the outcome tomorrow?*

I've sketched a framework that helps you to think about this question in
Figure 3. It shows that, as you think through a decision (1), you imagine

---

**Figure 3. A Decision is the Thought Process You Use to Determine How
Actions Lead to Outcomes.**

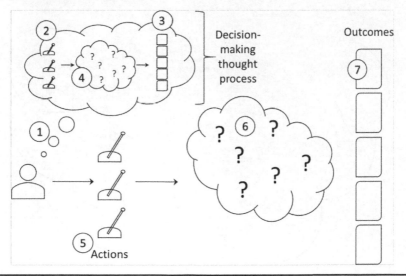

how your actions (2) will lead to outcomes (3) through a cause-and-effect chain of events (4). This chain of events can be difficult to understand. Then, based on this thought process, you take action(s) (5) in the real world, which leads through the actual cause-and-effect chain of events (6) to some outcome(s) over time (7). Your ability to match the decision to the reality (and to adapt your decision as the external environment changes, which I'll talk about below) is how you ultimately get what you want, avoiding unintended consequences.

Clearing the "cloud of decision fog" labeled with question marks in Figure 3 is how this book addresses the question above. As shown in Figure 4, a CDD replaces the ?s in this figure.

Simply put, a CDD is a map of how stakeholders in a decision see their actions leading to outcomes through a chain of events, calculations, or implications. Its primary goal is to represent how people *naturally* think about a decision: a diagram of what would otherwise be explained in words.

Figure 4. How a CDD Removes the ?s, Clarifying the Path From Actions to Outcomes.

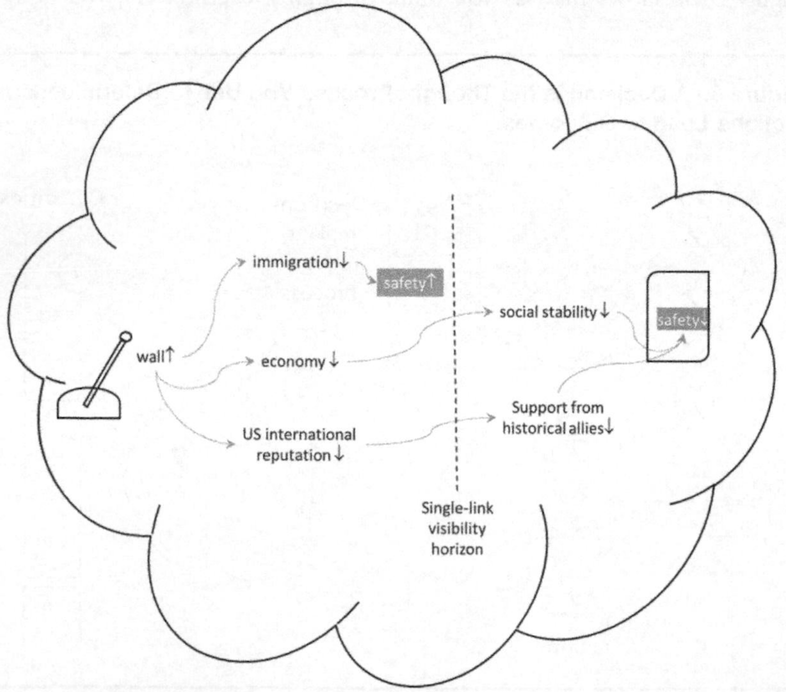

As I'll explain in more detail below, I consider CDDs a major breakthrough: not because they are original (90% of how a CDD works builds on the shoulders of great thinkers), and not because they are perfect (we'll probably be updating how CDDs are designed as DI matures). Rather the CDD is important because it (a) is focused on human decision makers (and any future design must maintain the simplicity and understandability of each part of the diagram); (b) captures a widespread archetype for how people think about decisions; and (c) acts as a framework into which advanced technologies can be inserted, so as to work hand in hand with the natural thought process used by decision makers.

The value of a CDD is a key insight of this book:

> **Key Insight #2:** A causal decision diagram (CDD) provides individual understanding, team alignment, and technology insertion points for decisions in complex environments.

CDDs are explained more below, and in detail in Chapter 2 and Chapter 4, which teaches you how to draw them. In my work and that of several other organizations, CDDs are core to DI.

An important side note: in this book, the meaning of "decision" is different than "deciding that," for example "deciding that" the Earth is round, or "deciding that" you are standing in front of me. My focus here is on decisions regarding actions that lead to outcomes. So "decision" here means "the decision to take some action," not "the decision to reach some conclusion." Conclusions are important, of course, but are well covered by centuries of work, much more so than actions based on those conclusions

> **Key Insight #3:** "Deciding that" a particular fact is true requires a fundamentally different activity than "*deciding to take an action* with the goal of reaching some outcome," which depends on those facts, but goes considerably beyond them.

LINK IS ABOUT DECISION INTELLIGENCE: A FOCUSING LENS ON COMPLEXITY

Before diving into the nuts and bolts of DI, CDDs, and the technologies and disciplines they unify, let's step back to understand where they fit in to the history of artificial intelligence (AI) and related fields.

"Grand unifying theories" of intelligence were attempted by the early AI pioneers, who focused on logic as the best way to represent human thought. Core to their way of representing our knowledge were facts and mechanisms for representing them, like "if George is an elephant (fact) and all elephants are gray (logical statement), then George is grey (deduction)."

These initiatives were missing two key insights: (1) that intelligence is better represented "subsymbolically" (e.g., at a more primitive level than verbal words/symbols); and (2) that reaching decisions that lead to outcomes is at least as (and some would say more) important as facts that lead to conclusions or answers.

When I started graduate school at Rutgers University in 1996, the AI-focused computer science department used symbolic AI exclusively. I am grateful that supported my "rebel" position to study neural networks instead. Modern AI (and the research of most of my former colleagues) is now 99% subsymbolic: it has broken through the first limitation listed above.

DI is a rebellion against the second limitation:

> **Key Insight #4:** DI shifts our focus beyond science and systems (including AI) that "answer questions," "provide insights," or "make predictions" to those that help us make to decisions that guide actions, which lead to outcomes. Answers, insights, and predictions are usually necessary, but not sufficient, for connecting actions to outcomes.

> **Key Insight #5:** The DI focus is on natural to humans, which leads to better human–machine collaborations, since we make thousands of decisions every day.

Many decisions are based on habit ... some are based on weighing pros and cons ... and the most complex ones come from humans imagining how our actions will play out through a chain of cause-and-effect, through time. "Knock-on effects" ... "blowback" ... "chain of events" ... "vicious cycle"... "virtuous cycle" ... these are all phrases we use in language, but we don't yet have a disciplined way of talking about decisions, nor of connecting them to data and technologies like AI.

Starting with a decision may seem too simple at first to solve complex problems. But it turns out that using decisions as a starting point leads to a great leap forward. Referring back to Figure 4 (and as will be shown in many similar diagrams throughout this book) when we build a CDD, we identify those factors in the chain from actions to outcomes.

The technology, tools, methodologies, and ways to draw pictures that help us to understand the winding path that an action you might take sets in motion through reality are neither too ambitious as to be intractable, nor too simple to be useless outside of the lab. So decisions are like "Goldilocks": neither too small nor too large, but "just the right sized lens" to solve the most important problems.

This focus is huge. It means we are freed from modeling *all* of human thinking or *everything* about a situation. Instead, we can be practical: given what I face today, how can I better understand the path from my actions to my outcomes? And, importantly, to be useful, this approach doesn't have to lead us to a *perfect* understanding; it just needs to be *better* than we've done before. And trust me, based on interviews with hundreds of decision makers over a decade of work, I've discovered there is huge room for improvement. If you're a data scientist you might be under the mistaken impression that the bigger the impacts of a decision, the more diligence is used in making it. As I'll describe in more detail later on, the opposite is often true. Chapter 5 lists the explosion of possibilities created by this new perspective.

DI connects human decision makers to the most powerful technologies, as well as social and management sciences that turn invisible decisions into visible ones, as I'll describe in more detail in Chapter 3. It builds on the shoulders of giants: thinkers like Buckminster Fuller, Douglas Englebart, Norbert Wiener, Daniel Kahneman, Gregory Bateson, John von Neumann, and W. Edwards Deming. DI owes its roots to visionaries like Mahatma Gandhi and Adam Smith, and to technologies and disciplines that have previously been separate but are here united in a common framework: complex systems, behavioral economics, cognitive science, neurobiology, ML, and more.

The Link: Core to Decisions

Within the complexity of these disciplines, there is a universal organizing principle: the cause-and-effect *link*. As you'll learn in this book, we can easily create pictures of decisions out of these links and then share, improve, and supercharge those pictures with technology and science.

> **Key Insight #6:** Even if we do nothing more than drawing a CDD together, the alignment we achieve between our mental models of a situation can have tremendous value.

This book is a road map to solving the hard problems. It is about reclaiming power in a new world where technology has accelerated beyond our ability to understand or effectively control it. No, we're not talking about the self-replicating robot apocalypse. The reality is harder to understand, but immeasurably more important. My mission in *Link* is to begin to turn attention away from the post-apocalyptic fiction of AI problems to the important ones, to shift our priorities from the next app to the next meal ... from ending a chat session to ending a war.[1]

UNDERSTANDING CAUSE-AND-EFFECT *LINKS*

If you listen to a news program tonight, pay attention to the causal link words broadcasters might use: *The man who opposed ethnic diversity wished to make his feelings known, so he argued with the immigrant.* Or *The immigrant wished to make a point, so he sought out a protest group to confront.* Decisions by these two people had both immediate — single link — effects and, as I write these words, are also playing out in a series of multi-link consequences, both intended and unintended. For these gentlemen, these longer-term and remote consequences will certainly dominate any immediate value of communicating their opinion, as I explore in more detail below.

A side note: experts might observe that many of the links in a CDD are not, strictly speaking, based on cause and effect. Some are simply calculations, such as net profit that is calculated by subtracting revenues from costs. The reason for this is that CDDs were designed to match, as closely as possible, how people describe their decisions, and people don't naturally make this distinction as they describe a decision. So a simple CDD that doesn't distinguish between a cause and a calculation can have great value. As you get more sophisticated, you'll learn that the type of cause-and-effect link (whether a "real cause" or just a calculation or correlation) will determine how that *Link* operates in practice.

From Single- to Multi-link Thinking

House prices always go up, so invest in mortgages; there are too many illegal drugs in our society, so make the penalties for using drugs stiffer; many people don't have enough to live on, so tax the rich more and give more to the poor.

Each of these statements might be considered "single-link" reasoning. In contrast, cognitive scientist George Lakoff points out that a single-link conclusion may be different than a multi-link one:

> *Immigrants are flooding in from Mexico [...] build a wall to stop them. For all the immigrants who have entered illegally, just deport them [...] The cure for gun violence is to have a gun ready to directly shoot the shooter [...] All this makes sense to direct causation thinkers, but not those who see the immense difficulties and dire consequences of such actions due to the complexities of systemic causation.*
>
> — George Lakoff [17][2]

Some might argue that this direct-consequence reasoning is limited and that, for example, "build a wall" has a number of downstream consequences that aren't captured in a single link and which actually lead to the opposite outcome. Figure 5 illustrates these two points of view. By drawing a CDD like this, we make explicit the difference between these two rationales for a

---

Figure 5. A Simple Causal Decision Diagram (CDD) That Shows How Multi-link Thinking May Lead to Different Expected Outcomes from an Action Than Single-link Thinking Does.

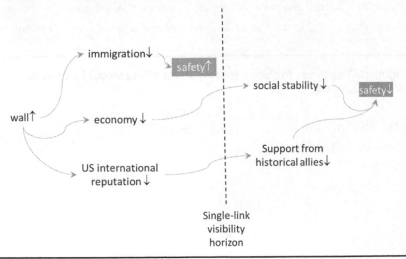

---

decision, allowing people who initially disagree to unpack their thinking, thereby increasing the likelihood of reaching agreement.

Understanding how our actions lead to consequences — both intended and unintended — is essential in a complex world. Yet, outside of academics and engineering, we lack even the most basic language for talking about multiple links like the ones shown above.

Direct-causation thinking is a consequence of making decisions using words and text alone, and not using pictures to illustrate chains of events. Text and verbal language may be adequate for a linear world, but quickly reach a dead end when used to explain complex systems; it is simply impossible to keep track of all the elements in a diagram like the one in Figure 5 when they are invisible or shown in a linear text document. Indeed, many cognitive biases — common thinking mistakes — can be explained by the fact that we use language to solve problems that are much better understood visually.

A telecom company tells its employees, "This year, our priority is customer experience. Everything we do must connect to that." If a company took this seriously, it might just send everyone a free car (this is, of course an exaggeration to illustrate the point).

A deeper, multi-link, analysis is essential to understand the trade-off between the positive and negative effects of this policy decision. This example illustrates the first of several classic decision making mistakes that I'll review in this book, called "false proxies." This pattern is shown in Figure 6: a model that only focuses on "customer satisfaction" as the goal shows that giving away free cars to everyone is a good idea. This doesn't

Figure 6. The Proxy Problem: Missing Parts of the Model Lead to the Wrong Conclusion.

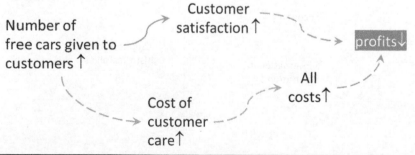

take into account the connection between happy customers and a net profit, which of course depends on the cost of those cars, which will, of course, be prohibitive.

Another example is that the US military changed the formula it uses to compensate officers for housing from a flat per-person rate to one based on the number of roommates, thinking it would save on costs without impacting its servicemen. What the military didn't foresee: there is now no incentive to economize. No longer can the service person pocket the difference between the fixed rate and the lower-priced housing they locate. This "use it or lose it" decision pattern is widespread [18].

Says serial entrepreneur Jim Casart:

> I love the Decision Intelligence idea of taking my strategic ideas on virtual test flights. Virtual crashes are much less painful than the real thing. My Boards appreciate the difference. [19]

Another example is that well-meaning international development initiatives that inject millions of dollars into a region create a familiar pattern of quick expansion followed by failure. "Stop trying to save the world" says an article in The New Republic, which encourages a deeper understanding of system interdependencies [20].

Solving the Tragedy of the Commons

One of the most important multi-link decision patterns is one called the "tragedy of the commons": the failure to see that a contribution to a common good will, in the long run, provide a benefit to that society and so, ultimately, to individuals.

Some examples: Raise the minimum wage, and workers will have more to spend, which improves the economy and ultimately makes the society wealthier. Alternatively (or in addition), create a new policy that lowers taxes on profits and income, which leads to companies having more to invest, which will lead workers to have more disposable income, which again improves society at large.

Or, invest in a better legal system in a war-ravaged country, which improves citizens' trust in the rule of law, which decreases preemptive violence, which stabilizes businesses, which improves the tax base, providing funds for further legal improvements.

Or, reduce your company's carbon emissions, which benefits the environment, stabilizing the economy, and creating an asset for your great-grandchildren. Another possible approach: create a policy to deregulate businesses, which allows them to cut costs, which will create competitive pressures, which will lead to reduced emissions.

Each of these actions is a step that will, though costly in the near term and within a limited scope of influence, potentially create a greater benefit in the longer run. The failure to navigate these long-term cause-and-effect chains effectively is leading to tragedies worldwide. And a few relatively simple techniques, which I describe more below, go a long way. We can — and we must — do better.

EVIDENCE-BASED DECISION MAKING: WHAT'S BROKEN

The *Harvard Business Review* correctly calls the modern organization a "Decision Factory" [21]. However, most do not use a consistent formal process for decision making; the factory is systematically broken (Figure 7) [22].

> **Key Insight #7:** If you are a data scientist or in a similar position separated from the ranks of senior executives, you might be under the impression that the more impactful (on factors like lives, dollars, jobs, and health) the decision, the more diligence is used in making it.

Figure 7. Only 14% of Organizations Generally Follow a Formal Decision Making Methodology.

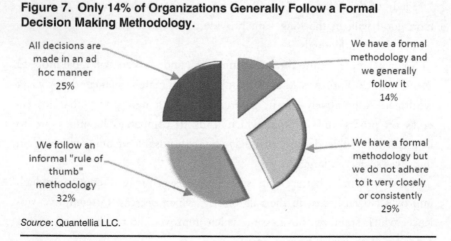

Source: Quantellia LLC.

Indeed, for reasons discussed in this book, more often than not, the opposite is true.

There are deep reasons for this failure. As shown in Figure 3 and Figure 6, making good decisions is about tracing a causal chain from actions to outcomes. Yet, despite this central role in the most human of all cognitive processes, causal models have been systematically ignored in the history of psychology (where they are called *prospective models*[3]), cognitive science, artificial intelligence, and other fields. Judea Pearl explains this history in *The Book of Why*. An excerpt:

> *We live in an era that presumes that big data is an answer to all of our problems [...] yet data are profoundly dumb. Data can tell you that the people who took a medicine recovered faster than those who did not take it. But they can't tell you why. Maybe those who took the medicine did so because they could afford it, and would have recovered just as fast without it. Over and over again in science and in business, we see situations where mere data are not enough.*
>
> — Judea Pearl and Dana Mackenzie [23]

For these reasons and more, there is not a standard way of drawing and sharing maps of decisions, and using this standard framework to integrate with other humans and with technology. This is the essence of DI. And this gap is so essential that filling it creates an explosion of new possibilities, which are described in Chapter 5. Setting a spark to this explosion is the aim of this book and is central to solutions that have been simultaneously realized by thousands worldwide who share many elements of the consensus at the end of the chapter.

WHO IS USING DECISION INTELLIGENCE?

Some organizations have begun to use a common framework for decision making. Some examples (some of which are described in more detail in later chapters), are as follows:

- A Canadian telecommunications company looking to build an "adaptive" and intelligent Internet by reducing its 11-figure spend on network assets.

- NASA's Frontier Development Laboratory, which built a Deflector Selector DI tool to weigh options for how to avert an asteroid inbound toward earth.

- An Australian bank that needs to make better decisions about loans by understanding how its risk exposures are connected to a common underlying cause, thereby substantially increasing its exposure should that risk materialize.

- The city sustainability manager who needs to make traffic and policy decisions that will drive his city toward a massive reduction in its carbon footprint.

- The world's largest financial organization who saved millions per year using a DI solution on a 53-country project.

- An NGO team in Liberia looking to reverse the vicious cycle of war.

- A Silicon-valley based open source team using DI to match disabled workers to their "perfect job."

- The mobile telephone company trying to decide how much to invest in its app store developers.

- An American health care company helping its clients to reduce the terrible costs of failed medical devices.

- A technology firm that is using DI to optimize political volunteer actions to engender trust instead of using propaganda messages to engender fear and anger.

So how are these organizations going about formalizing the decision making process? To help you to understand what I'm talking about, in the following section I'll describe one of the first projects I helped to lead in this space.

DECISION INTELLIGENCE IN PRACTICE: A TECHNOLOGY TRANSFORMATION EXAMPLE

Leaving the airport in our rental car, we saw a hot-air balloon perched on the roof of the European corporate headquarters[4] where we were to meet the following day. Arriving from various US locations, members of our five-person team were notified of a massive environmental protest against our client. As we checked into the hotel, our phones alerted us with a text: the meeting had been diverted to downtown. Tomorrow, it told us, please keep a low profile and enter through the shipping entrance at the back. This was going to be interesting.

Our team is proud that we solve the hardest problems. This one would be a particular challenge, as the company's external impact on the environment was looping back to create a reputational impact, leading to today's protest. This was on the top of the already overwhelming complexity our client faced: our mission going in was to help manage a massively complex world-wide project, deploying new technology in dozens of countries, juggling relationships with hundreds of companies in its supply chain, all while seeking to optimize spending inside a complex cost accounting structure. We were not to act as process modelers, financial modelers, data analysts, or program managers. Instead, our goal was to help to model a complex *decision*.

Our client was a large multinational. To manage just one facet of its business (say, technology requirements) requires a team of hundreds, so the company has — wisely — decomposed responsibility into many departments. The size of these departments is large enough that each has its own internal terminology, data sources, culture, and processes.

Unfortunately, however, the departmental decomposition did not reflect the reality of the problem this company faced: as in many organizations, there were complex interdependencies with ill-defined interfaces between these groups. Finance didn't fully understand technology. Technology didn't understand how supply chain impacted its constraints. The connection between finance and supply chain decisions wasn't modeled. And if, as sometimes happens, there is a moment of clarity, then something changes and the fog of complexity descends again.

Our task in this project was to help the company to reason about these between-department interdependencies, so as to maximize the benefit of a multibillion dollar transformation project.

We used a CDD.

A dozen people from various departments joined our meeting the first day. Every stakeholder group was represented. I walked the team through the key parts of a CDD: *outcomes*, *goals*, *constraints*, decision *levers* (which correspond to actions), *dependency* links, and *externals*. I asked them to focus on "structure before data," because the situation was so complicated that any mention of data at this stage would make the problem too hard to understand.

By the time our week was done, we had filled the whiteboard four times over with model diagram elements.

A couple of weeks later, our first project deliverable was a set of CDDs that showed how the choices of the various groups interacted. A master CDD showed how scheduling decisions for this project impacted multiple departments and, ultimately, the company's bottom line.

Our client told us that simply the exercise of eliciting and creating this *single diagram*, which unified the mental models of dozens of project participants, was worth millions to the company. I can't show you the picture we drew, because it's still considered confidentially valuable. But it's important to realize that this is *not* a kind of diagram you've seen before: it is not a process map nor an entity-relationship diagram for a database, nor is it a flowchart or an object model.

> **Key Insight #8:** Interdependencies between departmental silos in a complex organization are often not well-understood, and so mapping them can create a lot of value.

I'll return to this project in the next chapter. But for now, let's step back again to understand the importance of projects like this one, and why they really are something new and valuable.

MAKING THE INVISIBLE VISIBLE

[...] we have developed the power of thinking so rapidly and one-sidedly that we have forgotten the proper relation between thoughts and events, words and things. Conscious thinking has gone ahead and created its own world [...] What we have forgotten is that thoughts and words are conventions, *and that it is fatal to take conventions too seriously.*

> – Alan W. Watts
> (*The Wisdom of Insecurity* [24])

The CDD is a decision "map" showing the important connections between actions and outcomes in an organization. It stands in stark contrast to text- or language-based decision tools like policy documents, analysis reports, or the evening news. The CDD is also intended to be neutral: a platform for collaboration and not persuasion. When done right, a CDD should not embody bias that leads to the "right' decision. Because a CDD is a more transparent representation, this is less likely but by all means not a certainty.

The next section describes why it's critical to move from these invisible spaces to a visual one.

The Intelligence of the Visual Spatial

Imagine me throwing a ball to you without warning. You'd reach to catch it, and you'll probably succeed. Now, consider the sophisticated processing your brain performed: you calculated the ball's parabolic trajectory, along with the angles and speeds of your shoulder, elbow, wrist, and fingers.

Now, imagine you're blindfolded, and I have to explain my throw in words. Chances are you won't catch the ball this time. This is the situation faced by many decision makers — we have unnecessarily limited our ability to communicate, because we are only using words. Until recently, words have been enough, before the world went global and complexity exploded.

This practice of creating a visual analog to previously invisible thought processes has deep roots, including W. E. Deming's process mapping and the Unified Modeling Language used for software design [25]. I'll introduce the practice of building these maps — called decision modeling — in the following sections and provide step-by-step instructions in Chapter 4. By shifting from text and language to the visual/motor space, DI brings this much smarter, older, and less error-prone [26] part of our brains to bear.

> **Key Insight #9:** By moving from invisible words and text to diagrams, we supercharge our ability to think about complex systems.

But the approach that is emerging goes well beyond visual maps. Indeed, the CDD serves as a "backbone" for evidence, predictions, ML, data, sensors, human expertise, and more.

> **Key Insight #10:** Organizing evidence-based decision making around a decision model is the best mechanism for integrating these technologies, because it is the most natural and familiar picture of how we naturally think through decisions.

The CDD Is the Right Scaffold

Imagine a pile of Christmas ornaments without a tree to hang them on … a body without bones … a house without a frame. When we ignore the decision archetype, this is the situation we face today and is the bane of decision making practices conversations or text to solve the important problems.

The vast majority of media, whether it be delivered on television or in print, can be viewed as a bucket of cause-and-effect statements, outcomes, and goals. These are elements of the decision archetype in the audio or text-based form. For me to explain a model to you, I unwind these elements in a linear, narrative structure. *Such a structure is fundamentally different from the world that it describes*, which operates in parallel and includes feedback loops and dynamic effects. Narrative structures (including this book) are by necessity linear: one thought follows another in time. But the world is anything but. So, as shown in Figure 8, there is massive information loss and distortion during this shift of representation.

The idea that a picture is worth a thousand words is nothing new. What is new here is the power of a shared pictorial language that visualizes and allows us to unambiguously share with others something that, until now, has only been internal to our own thoughts: the myriad of factors, and relationships between them, that we consider when we make decisions in a complex environment. In addition, as organizations, governments, and you make decisions in a complex world, learning about their components through text

Figure 8. Information Loss When Complex Situations are Translated through Linear Media.

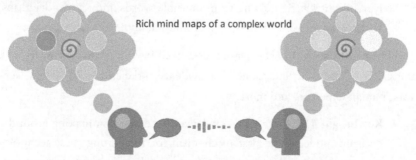

Rich mind maps of a complex world

Narrow, linear channel for verbal or written communication

alone and communicating them through words is creating a massive loss of information that can be overcome, in part, by using a visual metaphor.[5]

THE DI CONSENSUS

Again, the core *Link* question is:

> *If I make this decision, which leads to this action, in these circumstances, today, what will be the outcome tomorrow?*

Surrounding this question, there is an emerging consensus along the following lines:

- In the face of complexity, many people are simply giving up. They feel no *agency*: no ability to affect the future. And the second-order effects from this sense of impotence is potentially disastrous, as it increases susceptibility to despots and others promising easy fixes. A widespread understanding of how actions connect to outcomes has the potential to renew a sense of agency and optimism, to reverse widespread pessimism and to revolutionize democracy.

- A *discipline* that lets us answer this question in systematic, disciplined, ways has universal value.

- These systems cannot be limited to highly trained experts. They must be *democratized* and ubiquitous, inviting citizen contribution.

- Without such a discipline, the frequency of *unintended consequences* will become untenable.

- As humans think through questions like the one above, there is a *universal mental model archetype*: we imagine cause-and-effect paths going forward into the future, a "mental simulation."

- If we create *visual maps* of these mental models, we can *collaborate* more effectively.

- We are much smarter and much better at collaborating, if we use a visual representation, because we can leverage the visual and motor cortex of our *brains*. (This is why we can't build an airplane without a diagram (or

CAD system), or why endlessly scanning tables of data tells us nothing, but a mere glance at a chart is instantly meaningful.)

- If we think of these maps as *engineered artifacts*, we can then borrow many capabilities from engineering domains, including design, quality assurance, continuous improvement, rigorous review, and collaborative creation.

- *Computers* can help us to run these mental *simulations*, when the complexity of the situation becomes too complex for our brains working alone. (Simulation is why airplanes don't crash, and the Apollo 13 astronauts made it home.)

- These systems must invite multiple points of view. This *diversity* is critical to solving the hard problems (and the lack of such diversity is part of why we haven't solved them, so far).

- Understanding the *interdependencies* between departments, disciplines, and global challenge domains (like water, inequality, and poverty) is an important unsolved problem.

- Any computer system that helps us in this way must be *simple* to use, and *match our mental models* as closely as possible. Granny and the grandkids: they must both understand it.

- These simulations are based on *complex systems* dynamics and often include feedback loops, attractors, phase shifts, and transient effects.

- *Artificial Intelligence* and *Big Data* can inform the *causal links* in such a model. This is how the most advanced and important technologies today can be used to solve the most important problems we face. Not to do so is a travesty.

- Facebook and other online tools encourage *conversation*. There is a widespread hunger for a platform – as easy to use as Facebook – that goes *beyond conversation* to helping organize *actions* (not just ideas and words) that lead to outcomes (in the world, not just on your Smartphone).

- Creating these maps is a natural next frontier for *journalism* and is the basis for a *new mythos* in storytelling, especially science fiction.

- Much of this is *not new*: fields like decision analysis, cybernetics, complex systems, and more are all essential building blocks, some of which have long and rich histories.

- This is fundamentally different from, and complementary to, *data visualization*. DI gives us "data from the future" [27].

WHY "DECISION INTELLIGENCE?"

Some call us "systems thinkers," some "decision analysts," and for a while I called it "decision engineering." But many have found these names too limiting. As a technologist, I have been saying "decision intelligence," and over the years since creating this term (simultaneous with a number of others, I've since learned), there are now consultants, software vendors, NASA's FDL, and more who use this name, so I think it's going to stick.

ABOUT ME

A computer programmer since high school in the 1970s, I have three computer science degrees, two in AI. Between my academic and analyst careers, I have been building ML systems for over 30 years, and running DI projects for eight of them. I invented one of the core ML methods, called ML transfer [28] and wrote the seminal book in this space, *Learning to Learn*, with Sebastian Thrun [29]. My teams and I have built systems for dozens of organizations, including the Human Genome Project [30] and the US government [31].

ABOUT *LINK*

Why do you watch the news? Why do you go to school, or talk to your colleagues? More often than not, it's to gather bits of information: facts, recommendations, cause-and-effect links ("when Johnny went to private school he was so miserable," "Every time I've launched a new product in India, it's gone exceptionally well," and more). And why do you want that information? Usually it's to make decisions! But for complex decisions, where your actions have an effect at a distance or forward in time, things go off kilter: the assumption is that you can remember enough facts to make good decisions in many situations and that your brain is good at assembling that information. It's not. But it can be. This book explains how.

Link is written for four primary audiences:

(1) *Visionary Thinker*: You're interested in the future and you care about how to translate ideas into actions. You may wish to skip Chapter 4 which you might find too detailed.

(2) *Leader*: You know that decisions could be better and suspect that some combination of data, AI, economics, complex systems, warm data, or more might be helpful. *Link* connects these technologies and disciplines to value: whether it be revenue or public outcomes, or many goals that must be balanced.

(3) *AI expert:* This book provides a view into the future of ubiquitous AI. You may particularly enjoy Chapter 6, which describes new sub-specialties that are emerging which bridge data and algorithms to actions and value.

(4) *Educator: Link* can be used as a text to help understand how AI fits into modern organizations, along with how to bridge from use cases to technology and human expertise. It is also an important reference in political science, economics, and philosophy. For you, Chapter 4 may be the most valuable; the methodology described there can form the basis of a semester-long course during which you model and analyze multiple decisions. An instructor's guide is also planned.

Or, you might already be a "member of the tribe." I've been developing this field for about nine years now. During this time, I kept running into people who, though they were strangers, have glimpsed the same underlying solution. It's like the parable of the blind men and the elephant: "What a big snake," says the first blind man, feeling the trunk. "What a sturdy tree," says another, touching the elephant's leg. "A good rope," says the third, regarding the tail. "Material for a sturdy cloak," says the fourth, touching the ears. At some point, they realize the elephant is not merely separate parts; rather, it is a single organism: a complex system. How exciting it is to meet these fellow tribe members! Maybe you're one of us already, or maybe by reading this book you can join us.

Link has four main purposes:

(1) To help you to use DI to supercharge whatever you do: How to take the "invisible idea" of a decision shown in Figure 3 out of your head and

into a drawing, so you can share it with others, align your understanding of a situation, and continually adapt and improve it.

(2) To help you to use CDDs as the scaffold for integrating expertise from other people and "if this then that" *Links* that come from statistics, artificial intelligence, ML, complex systems, and many other fields.

(3) To capture in one place the breakthroughs and insights from the DI ecosystem so far, "moving the needle" as we crystallize and unify our work toward the solutions renaissance that is a necessity needed in a complex world.

(4) To inspire and catalyze the Solutions Renaissance, which I introduced above.

BOOK OVERVIEW

Chapter 2 next describes the root concept of many of the insights here: by treating decisions as artifacts that we can *design* and *engineer*, we gain critical important insights in being able to handle greater complexity.

You will probably be surprised to learn that AI, ML, data science, and many other of the most successful technologies today don't help with choosing the right *actions that lead to an outcome*. In contrast, fields like ML provide *answers to questions* like "Given this set of data about a patient, what is their likely prognosis?" or "Where are the faces in this image?" These fields are sometimes necessary, but not on their own sufficient, to get from actions to outcomes. Chapter 3 surveys several of these other fields that are part of the overall DI picture that I introduced in Figure 1.

Chapter 4 gives practical steps to model your own complex decisions. It includes examples of DI deployments along with best practices and classic mistakes.

Shifting to a decision-centric view creates an explosion of extensions and implications. Chapter 5 is a quick review of these possibilities.

Finally, Chapter 6 looks to the future, especially how the DI ecosystem is crystallizing and some of the important developments on the horizon.

A side note: this book is *not* about a review of techniques to make better decisions. Although I'll describe some of these along the way, *Link* is, in contrast, about placing decisions in a new, more central position in how we think about the world: as the "glue" that binds many disciplines into the solutions renaissance.

So join us (you already have!), and let's get started. Note that each chapter is written to be stand-alone, so you can skip around or read sequentially.

NOTES

1. Science fiction authors are paying attention to DI, and there is an emerging set of archetypes related to it which PJ Manney calls *The New Mythos*. So, Hollywood has some new AI fodder today. More about this is in Chapter 5.

2. For Lakoff's "systemic causation", I say "multi-link thinking."

3. See [191] for a great review of the reason for this.

4. All client details in this book have been modified to ensure confidentiality.

5. [223] provides a catalog of visual archetypes that may be useful for the more artistically inclined CDD creator.

CHAPTER 2

BREAKING THROUGH THE COMPLEXITY CEILING

At desks and in meeting rooms, every day of their working lives, knowledge workers hammer away in decision factories. Their raw materials are data, either from their own information systems or from outside providers. They produce lots of memos and presentations full of analyses and recommendations. They engage in production processes—called meetings—that convert this work to finished goods in the form of decisions.
— Roger L. Martin (Rethinking the Decision Factory [21])

As I introduced in Chapter 1, a causal decision diagram (CDD) acts as scaffolding to connect technologies and humans:

Key Insight #11: None of these pieces of decision intelligence (DI) are new. What's new is the glue.

Figure 1 showed some technologies and disciplines that can be combined to solve hard problems. The arrow labeled (3) there captured the idea of integrating them into a common framework.

In the remainder of this section, I'll describe an example of how this integration can be done. Although the example is for a bank's customer service division – which may sound a little boring if this isn't your business – it illustrates some essential characteristics of such systems that are usually overlooked yet are incredibly powerful, including intangibles and feedback loops. This same kind of analysis is applicable to many arenas, including climate change, power plant management, decisions about where to build solar panels, and much more.

A few years back, my company was looking for a new bank. My uncle was happy with Ward Bank[1], and it was the preferred bank for one of our investors, so I considered it as one of my options, and switched our company's accounts there. My uncle and my investor's happiness and recommendation were a big part of my reason for moving – they saved me time and effort doing due diligence myself, allowing me to effectively "piggyback" off their experience.

The same pattern played out a second time as I later chose Ward Bank for my personal bank, as did, subsequently, my niece and business partner. All our positive experiences caused a chain of events that ultimately led to three new personal customers and one new business customer, as shown in Figure 9.

You can imagine that, if this pattern was repeated, it could spell success not just for banks, but for many businesses. A satisfied customer's likelihood to recommend (L2R) it to others is essential for widespread success in many industries.

If a company wishes to take this pattern seriously, and to improve its L2R, how can it get started? In a world where data are plentiful, it is now possible to measure and assess this likelihood as a number associated with each customer, called their L2R score.

L2R can create a snowball effect: if you have ten customers and only one in five can recruit a new customer every six months, your customers will

Figure 9. The Chain of Recommendations around Me that Generated Some New Customers for My Bank.

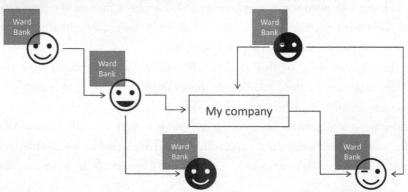

begin to grow slowly and then they will take off. As shown in Figure 10, below, these ten customers will grow to over 20,000 after year seven from this effect alone!

This pattern of rapid growth can be explained by a portion of a CDD like the one in Figure 11.

Figure 10. Recommendations Create Big Growth over Time.

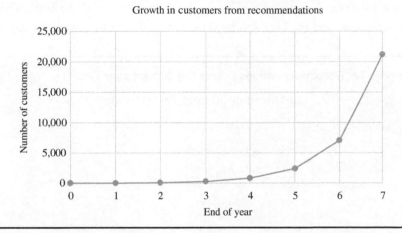

Growth in customers from recommendations

Figure 11. The More Customers We Have, and the Higher the Number of Recommendations Per Person, the Faster We'll Grow.

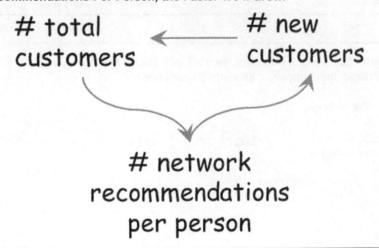

Increasing the number of customers drives more recommendations, which in turn drives more customers. The higher the L2R, the faster the growth. Figure 12 shows that a very small change – from one in five customers creating a recommendation to an L2R of one in four – leads to huge additional growth: now there are close to 120,000 customers by the end of year seven from recommendations alone.

So, if a small increase in L2R makes such a big difference, how can a company make it bigger? In my case, this was impacted by my experience as a customer – I was greeted at the door when I entered the bank, there was no wait, and the banker offered me coffee. Figure 13 shows this impact

Figure 12. Recommendations Create Big Growth over Time.

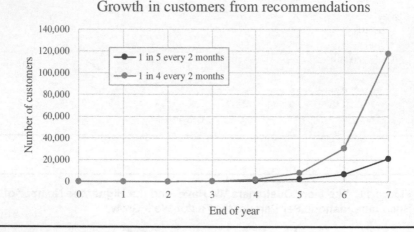

Figure 13. We Can Influence the L2R with Better Marketing, or by Activities that Improve Customer Experience.

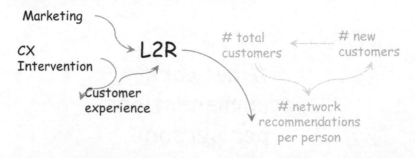

Figure 14. Adding Recommendation Effectiveness to the L2R Model.

of a customer experience decision on my experience, which in turn influenced my L2R.

When I make a recommendation to a friend, their likelihood to change to my bank is also dependent on their own experience as they walk in the door or call the bank. So the investment in customer experience has a "double dipping" effect, as shown in Figure 14.

Using only what is shown in this picture, a bank might be motivated to max out my L2R with an even better experience. How about a free coffee maker? How about a free car whenever I opened an account? Obviously, this would be impractical, as I illustrated in Figure 6. The reason is that these interventions come at a cost, as shown in Figure 15.

Figure 16 goes on to show how costs are subtracted from revenues, which depend on the number of customers, to determine net revenues, or profit.

Figure 17 shows labels on the lines in this figure using squares. One color of square represents those links that can be calculated with a bit of math. For instance, net revenue is just a subtraction: gross revenues minus total cost.

Another color of square represents which of these links could be supported by a machine learning (ML) model. For instance, ML is a great

Figure 15. L2R Interventions Come at a Cost.

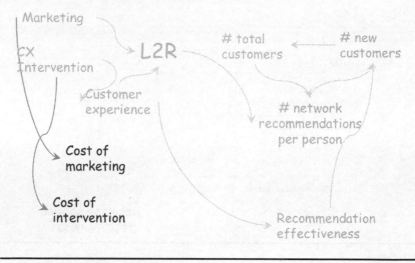

Figure 16. Costs Are Weighted against Revenues to Determine Total Net Revenues (Profit).

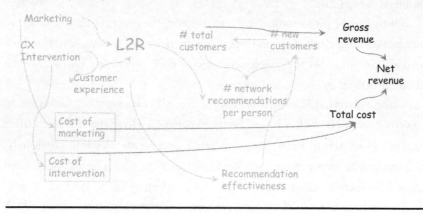

approach to learn which kinds of marketing, to which kinds of people, affect L2R, in what way.

Finally, another square color labels links that involve what have traditionally been viewed as "soft" links; exactly how much does that coffee influence my satisfaction (experience) at the bank? And then, how does my level of satisfaction affect the degree to which my recommendation is effective?

Figure 17. How Math, Machine Learning, and "Soft" Factors Underlie the Bank L2R Model.

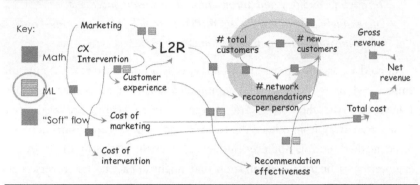

The Ward Bank story illustrates several important points, which are relevant far beyond this limited example. Whether we are talking about company, individual, or government decisions that impact climate, democracy, or business, the following are often true:

> **Key Insight #12:** Feedback loops dominate the impact of decisions in many arenas, much more than precise values of data.

The feedback loop highlighted in Figure 17 (the thick circular gray arrows) represents a pattern that underlies the most successful companies, the most successful economic initiatives, and more. When designed right, these loops lead to a "winner-takes-all" effect that leads to market dominance [32]. These are called nonlinearities (a simple way to think of why is because the shape of the curves in Figure 12 were not lines), and are only beginning to be well understood in many domains.

> **Key Insight #13:** "Soft" cause-and-effect links aren't taken as seriously as "hard" ones like dollars, but they often matter more.

"Soft factors" — also called "intangibles" — are those aspects of a decision making process that are hard to measure and/or relate to psychological factors like brand awareness, morale, empathy, customer satisfaction, or happiness.

Economist and game theory expert Ruth Fisher says that:

> *People tend to shy away from intangibles because they're difficult to measure, but since you only manage what you measure, even a*

bad proxy can be much more effective than no proxy. Also, in today's world, the hard stuff is increasingly becoming optimized through technology and automation. This means success is increasingly determined by the soft stuff, which is less obvious—but not impossible—to manage and measure [33].

In modern organizations, by and large, only a few soft factors, if any, are emphasized. In my work with telecommunications companies over the years, I have observed that groups in charge of these factors are also often sequestered away from others; the team in charge of customer satisfaction is given neither control, nor even influence, over the decisions made by the engineering or financial organization that might impact it. The reverse may also be true; an initiative that may drive sales through increased L2R may not be communicated adequately to the engineering department, who might then be caught off guard.

Key Insight #14: Soft factors within feedback loops are often the most influential on an organization's success, yet are systematically ignored.

Soft factors inside feedback loops are the most common "invisible" pattern driving big growth. Consider the "Starbucks Experience"; it's well understood that Starbucks can charge more for a cup of coffee because of its brand.

What you are paying for is not the coffee, but rather the experience that Starbucks offers. Nowhere else will you get the barista who remembers your order, that smell you get when you open the doors or even the light jazz or ambiance you get from a Starbucks [34].

What's less well understood is that this brand experience sits within a feedback loop: the company reinvests in ambience-improving factors like employee education and benefits, which drive additional opportunities to raise prices even further.

Surprisingly, and despite its power, in my six years as a technology analyst interviewing hundreds of companies, an understanding of the power of soft-factor-driven feedback loops *wasn't mentioned once.* Although this dynamic may be taught in some advanced business schools and economics programs, there remains a wide gap between theory and practice, and an even larger chasm to jump before there are best practices for using data, AI, and DI to systematically understand them.

The diagrams above can look complicated at first glance, but each part is simple in isolation. Innovations that allow a larger group of people to easily understand these dynamics are essential. This will require great graphical design, good user experience (UX) analysis, and more.

THE ORIGINS OF THE CDD

Decision Intelligence has been co-invented dozens of times worldwide. Each of us in the "tribe" has our own narrative about how we felt the pain of the complexity problem that DI solves, and how we came to a solution.

My story started by working with Mark Zangari beginning in 2008. A friend of Mark's had complained that he'd spent an exorbitant amount of money building what was to him a simple model to calculate the right price for a telecom company's new offering. Mark and I thought we might start a company to solve this problem, so we began a series of interviews.

The response, however, was lukewarm — it was clear that the pricing problem was not widespread enough to justify a new software system. But we did hear a common thread in a few of our conversations, which went something like this:

> It's not pricing decisions, exactly, that are my problem, but rather decision making as a whole. There is a lot of data out there and we're just not using it. And boy is our management dumb sometimes.

So we pivoted our questions to ask about this more general decision making need. By the time we were done, we'd interviewed 61 people in companies and organizations worldwide, asking "If technology could solve one problem for you that it has not solved, what would it be?"

It was exciting to hear one version or the other of the same core DI question articulated by many of our respondents: "Help me to know how my decisions will lead to outcomes." Senior managers said, "There's all this new technology, but it's too hard to understand and we don't end up using it for our most important decisions."

The most sophisticated users of data in senior positions created a quarterly PowerPoint deck, full of graphs and statistics. The expectation is that the decision makers could assemble these data in their heads and somehow understand which of the actions they might take would lead to the best outcome. Technologists told us, "We have great algorithms, data, and evidence, but we're consistently being ignored in the board room." Yet, this technology hit a brick wall: unless the analysis could directly illuminate what the consequences of each decision option were, for example in a simple chart, it didn't make the cut.

HOW WE INVENTED THE CDD

So we asked our decision makers a second question: "Please tell us a story about a high-value decision you've made in the past." The answer to this question was a key insight along the development of DI. After listening to dozens of answers, we realized that there was a consistent pattern to the responses [22].

You can test our finding for yourself by asking a friend to explain a high-value decision to you, as we did in our research. Usually you'll find that:

> **Key Insight #15:** There is a common pattern to how people describe decisions in complex environments.

Usually, you'll hear the same key elements that are listed below.

Options or choices: What should they do? Apply to Harvard or Dartmouth for college? Invest in new features for our mobile phone or lower its price? Acquire this new company or that one? Give a loan to this company or not? Launch a new product line this year, or not? In DI, we call these "Decision **Levers**" to avoid confusion.

Outcomes: What will they measure to determine if they've been successful? "My annual salary," "How much stress I feel during college?" "How much I will pay for tuition per year?"

Goals: What measurement will be considered a success? "I'd like to have a high-paying job," "I'd like to avoid a high-stress college career," "I'd like to end up spending less than $10,000 per year on tuition."

Externals: "I only have $5,000 in the bank." "There is a loan program that may pay my whole way." "I've heard that Harvard is very stressful."

Cause-and-effect links: These may be positive:

If I go to Harvard, I think I could make a lot of friends [...] Having a lot of good friends can reduce the stress of college [...] Harvard has a great reputation on Wall Street [...] Going to an ivy league school with a good reputation on Wall Street can land me a great job.

These may also be negative:

Harvard is very expensive [...] If the school is expensive, I could be saddled with a lot of debt [...] Lots of debt after I graduate could make me unhappy.

These Links are the core of this book, and they are very closely aligned with Nora Bateson's "warm data" as I'll describe in Chapter 3.

Intermediates: These are aspects of the decision that come between the levers and outcomes. In the example given earlier, an intermediate might be "how much my choice of school enhances my reputation on Wall Street," or "amount that I pay for tuition over four years."

An *archetype*, according to the early twentieth-century psychologist and writer Carl Jung, is defined as "the contents of the collective unconscious" [35]. Jung discovered that there are patterns of thought that transcend cultures and persist through time, and are yet not fully realized: they are tacit, unconscious. The above elements, it appears, constitute a *decision archetype*: a pattern of thought that is universal and which is used for making decisions.

A CDD is how I draw the elements of this archetype. Its template is shown in Figure 18.

Figure 18. The Decision Archetype: A Template for the Causal Decision Diagram (CDD).

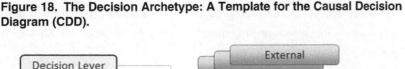
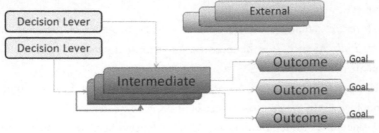

CDD EXAMPLES

The references below include videos, articles, and online demonstrations that show CDDs in more detail:

- [36] describes a model built by Bloomberg for cable telecom operators to use to make decisions as to where and when to build distributed power generation facilities, such as solar panels on a roof or an adjacent wind farm.

- [37] explores the impacts of donations to rule-of-law programs in Liberia. A screenshot is shown in Figure 20.

- [38] is a video that was used at the United Nations during the Forbes 400 conference to describe the value of investments in a health program in Liberia.

- Figure 19 shows a screenshot from [39] (follow the reference to experiment with an online interactive model).

I'll return to several of these examples in more detail in Chapter 4.

CDDs AS A FRAMEWORK FOR INTEGRATING OTHER TECHNOLOGIES

If we know that a cause has happened, how can we go about representing the effect in a computer? At its simplest, we might say "when poverty goes down, happiness goes up" − probably the simplest kind of qualitative cause-and-effect connection.

Or we might say "here's a graph that lets you know how well I will do in a particular job, based on my number of publications," as shown in Figure 21.

There are actually many ways to obtain the structure of the cause-and-effects *Link*. As such, it is the insertion point for many technologies. Some of them are named in Figure 22.

Using the CDD framework as illustrated earlier, DI bridges multiple technologies into the day-to-day needs of decision makers.

A side note: although a link in a CDD is labeled here to connect "cause" to "effect," these definitions often don't hold in a strict sense. A "cause"

Figure 19. Training Investment Decision Model.

By investing $1,000 in training that costs $100 per hour, 10 training hours can be purchased. Since the average skill level of the workforce before the investment is 3 (on a scale of 1-100), this can produce a skill level improvement of 10 (as measured on an assessment test with a scale of 1-10) for every training hour purchased, resulting in a total predicted skills improvement score of 100. Analysis of our historical data shows that this will avoid, on average, 0 days of project delay. Project delay days cost the company, on average, $3000 each. This means that the expected benefit from the $1,000 initial investment is $0, representing a net loss of $1,000.

Training Investment: $1,000

Cost per hour of training: $100

Average skill level today: 3

Cost of a day of project delay: $3,000

Copyright (c) 2015 Quantellia LLC.

Note: The interactive version is at http://www.di-everywhere.com/LPjs/BlogPr/ and is described in more detail in [39].

might be the cost of a product, and its "effect" may be the net profit. So this is just a simple calculation, in contrast to a real "cause" like pressing an accelerator pedal making a car move forward. As you can see by this example, the words, "cause" and "effect" are used loosely in this book: to match how people think about links, but not to match the underlying reality, which has more nuance. The reason for this choice is to avoid having to teach about all the different kinds of links before starting a decision mapping exercise with a team. The true distinctions between different kinds of cause-and-effect links don't even arise in some projects: simply understanding that one thing is dependent in some way on another thing, and that the team agrees about this dependency, is enough.

Figure 20. Decision Model Showing Cycle of Conflict in Liberia.

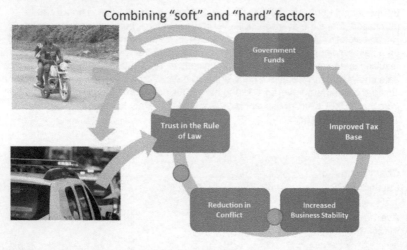

Figure 21. A "Sketch Graph" Showing the Relationship between the Number of Articles I've Published and My Suitability for a Particular Job.

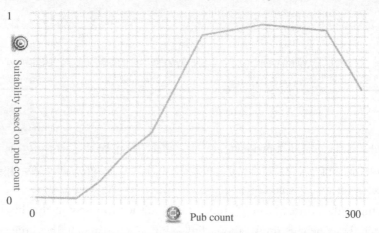

How DI Extends Machine Learning: A Simple Example

Returning to how links form an insertion point for other technologies, Figure 23 shows, for example, how the CDD template from Figure 18 can be extended to show that ML and/or statistical models might be injected at many of the cause-and-effect links in a decision.

Figure 22. Several Ways that We Might Represent the Information on a Cause-and-effect Link.

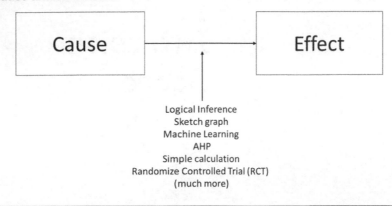

Logical Inference
Sketch graph
Machine Learning
AHP
Simple calculation
Randomize Controlled Trial (RCT)
(much more)

Figure 23. Schematic Diagram Showing that Machine Learning and/or Other Kinds of Models Can Support Many Elements of the Generic Decision Model.

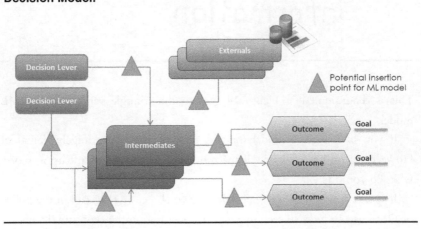

I'll describe ML models in more detail in Chapter 3, but for now you can think of an ML software system — called a *model* — that takes some input and produces some output.

For example, imagine we had a model that takes information about a computer system's activity as input, and produced a score between 0% and 100% indicating that the system security has been breached by a hacker, who is currently exploring the file system and possibly stealing information.

Figure 24. Schematic of a Machine Learning Model that Detects an Ongoing Hacker Intrusion.

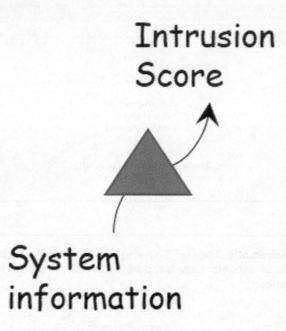

This is diagrammed in Figure 24, where the triangle represents the ML model.

If you had a good model for this task, it would be hugely valuable! However, it only goes so far: if the model produces a high intrusion score, what do you do next?

If you're a company, you might have two choices: (1) to call in the police or (2) to use an internal security team. Depending on the type and likelihood of the breach, there will be a different cost and benefit from each of these two options. Figure 25 is one diagram for this situation. It shows the full CDD surrounding this ML model, along with a second model that identifies the type of hack.

As you can see here, your two choices have different benefits and costs, with impacts on multiple outcomes. The cost cause-and-effect flows are shown in red; the benefits — in the form of reduced cost and risk from the security intrusion — are shown in green.

Figure 25. A Simple CDD.

The pattern shown here, where ML prediction models fit into a larger framework, applies in many domains. These include medicine ("What is the best treatment in these circumstances?"), customer care ("What should we say to this customer?"), capital expenditure ("Where should we build our next run of fiber optic cable"?), banking ("Which company should receive a bank loan?"), and many more. This leads to:

> **Key Insight #16:** Every ML system of value is ultimately used to support a decision and action of some sort, and so embedding one or more ML model(s) in a CDD is a helpful way to agree to those decisions and actions.

The simple diagram above is only the beginning, however, as many technologies beyond ML can support the causal links in the diagram, and the links can also form loops, creating "vicious" and "virtuous" cycles, as I'll be explaining in more detail in later chapters of this book.

THE CDD "A HA" MOMENT

There is a palpable moment in every DI meeting where the room takes a relaxing breath. No longer must everyone remember the invisible parts of a decision; they are now captured on the white board.

> **Key Insight #17:** When we capture a decision in a diagram, it has a big effect on our thinking: we no longer have to remember all of the invisible decision parts, and can now get creative about them.

Like other diagramming techniques of the past – whether a blueprint, business process model, software UML model, or CAD/CAM – a CDD delegates the mental work of keeping track of the pieces to paper and tools, freeing up human decision makers for the creative work that they do best. This also radically reduces the friction that comes from different, undocumented, understanding of a situation on the part of multiple stakeholders.

Of course, many organizations do make decisions using data, or using more advanced technology like AI, without a formal way to map it like the CDD. What's new here is a unifying framework for talking about those decision elements, instead of the mixed methods used today including verbal conversation, text documents, data visualizations, and more.

A TELECOM CUSTOMER CARE CDD EXAMPLE

Figure 26 is a CDD that shows how decisions about customer care can improve revenue. Like the one above, this shows how ML fits into DI. I built this model during a talk at the 2014 COMET Executive Summit – a meeting for telecommunications experts. I then presented the model as shown in the video at [40].

Figure 26. Telecom Call Center Decision Model.

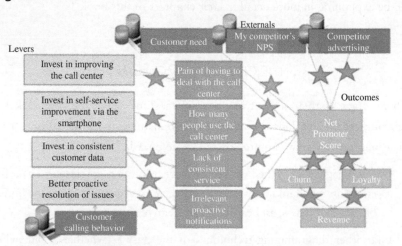

In the diagram, you'll see decision levers in yellow, outcomes in green, externals in red, and intermediates in blue. As I showed in Figure 25 for a security application, this diagram shows how ML sits within a larger decision framework. In this case there are multiple ML links, shown as stars. Some of them are:

- Predicting customer churn (loss of a customer to a competitor) likelihood.

- Predicting call center usage after an investment in self-service.

- Predicting the likelihood of a customer recommending our company to their friend, based on multiple factors like receiving consistent high-quality service, their loyalty as reflected on a customer survey, and other factors.

- Determining how investment in improving the self-service available via smartphones influence the number of call center users?

- How does call center volume impact net promoter score?

- How does an investment in making customer data more consistent improve the consistency of a customer's experience through multiple channels?

- … and much more.

DECISIONS BEFORE DATA

Spending too much of the wrong kind of effort on cleansing data in advance of decision modeling is a common mistake.

In practice, the data to build a ML system is often not available at first. The CDD remains useful as a diagram to align teams' understanding of the situation, as well as to drive analysis to determine where data is most valuable to analyze and prepare for ML. Even without data, the model can also be turned into a simulation by obtaining qualitative or quantitative formulas for the links which can stand in for the ML link, either temporarily or permanently.

The iterative nature of building models like this one deserves repeating: it is *not* necessary to have data before formally modeling decisions like these. Indeed, data can be a substantial distraction.

Key Insight #18: As we use a decision model, we gather data over time so that each link can represent our best understanding of how influence propagates. We can use *adaptive* learning techniques to continuously improve our ability to make decisions like these over time. *Indeed, we can launch a decision model initiative with no data at all. If we can gather data over time as we go forward, then all the better.*

The above insight is so important, and so much against current data-centric approaches to decision modeling, that it's worth reiterating in another way:

Key Insight #19: There is a "magic cycle" of DI, in which a CDD without data has value at the start; it gains information over time to become more and more powerful.

This view is in stark contrast to many AI and data-focused thought leaders who tend to *begin* with data, then look for a mechanism to use that data (e.g. AI), and only after that point start to ask detailed questions about the decisions that the data will drive. Working the other way is considerably more cost-effective if your goal is to solve problems (and buying or selling technology is, as it should be, secondary).

Key Insight #20: Data, technology, and AI must take a back seat to diligent understanding of the decisions that they support. There are thousands of projects worldwide today which do not bother to develop a collaborative, structured decision model, and thereby end up wasting tremendous resources.

Key Insight #21: Data management can be expensive — often unexpectedly so. Building a CDD helps to focus data management efforts on the parts of the decision that matter, thereby avoiding "gratuitous" data management effort, and getting to value faster and with lower risk.

THE COMPLEXITY CEILING

To achieve prosperous futures, we must update our mental models to embrace convergent outcomes rather than singular pathways. Our world is complex, fractal and often times chaotic, and the only

way that we can reach our aspirational goals is think in
simultaneous multiples and diverse possibilities, and pull from them
to ensure that we are adaptive, resilient and transformative.
How do we envision the best answers and right actions for today?
We must become creators of the future instead of sitting back and
letting fate determine what will happen to us.

— Frank Spencer/Yvette Montero Salvatico
(Kedge/The Futures School [1])

Imagine that you are a construction worker. Wearing your hard hat, you arrive to the new site on a crisp autumn morning, ready to begin your new job. You're excited, because this building is ambitious: it will stand out on the city's skyline as the tallest building.

The foreman addresses your team, "For this new kind of building, we're going to use a new approach. We're done with blueprints." Handing out thick folders to you and your colleagues, he says "please read this document. It will explain what we are going to build. There is a good explanation there, plus a lot of charts and graphs about our work."

This story is ridiculous. Of course, you wouldn't build a skyscraper — or, for that matter, anything complex like an airplane or rocket — without a blueprint (or its modern equivalent: a computer-assisted design tool). Yet, this is exactly what happens with the most complex decisions made at the largest companies and governments worldwide.

Take my friend Helmut. My former boss, and we'd kept in touch over the years. Helmut works for a European telecommunications company, on the CEO's advisory team, so he's involved in the company's most important decisions, affecting millions of subscribers worldwide. We've talked about decision intelligence over the years, and one day Helmut shared with me his standard decision making process. Every quarter or so, a colleague assembles a 200-slide PowerPoint presentation, with charts and graphs explaining aspects of his competition, new technology, and more. This is presented to the executive team, who then makes critical decisions: What new products should be offered? What companies should we acquire? What new technologies should we develop?

The problem is that it is a complete fiction that Helmut's team can assemble these charts inside their brains and synthesize the information they contain in any coherent way to make these decisions effectively. The idea of doing so is as ridiculous as expecting our construction worker to build a building without a blueprint.

To understand why, let's think about what a blueprint does for us. It shows how the individual pieces fit together to make a whole. It shows how the electrical systems might interfere with a plumbing line or a structural element of the building. Since a building is so tangible – something you can touch and move within – it's pretty obvious that you can't build anything much more complicated than a dog house without some basic diagrams like this. And, in recent years, we need much more computer support than a printed blueprint will provide: we use computer-assisted design (CAD) which allows us to see objects in three dimensions and to make them move (like the gears in a motor) to ensure that they fit correctly together.

Helmut's decisions are no less complex and no less in need of a structured way to "blueprint" them, than our skyscraper. But because a decision is *invisible*, it has, until recently, been less obvious that the blueprint is missing. And because those who head up organizations are those who were promoted in an environment of invisible decisions, there is a natural resistance to change, which has kept this suboptimal approach in place long past its "due by" date.

Breaking through the Complexity Ceiling

Helmut's story and many more like his demonstrate that organizational decision making has reached a *complexity ceiling*: the number of factors that come into play when making a major decision, along with their complexity, has exceeded our capacity to make the right choices (Figure 27). The amount of information that must be considered, the number of choices faced, and the way these can interact in unforeseen ways to produce disturbingly unexpected results, all accumulate to overwhelm the *ad hoc* techniques that most decision makers typically rely on.

Couple this with the seriousness of the consequences that may accompany bad decisions – today often measured not only in dollars, but in lives – and it becomes clear that huge risks are being taken based on justifications that are often far from sound.

Figure 27. DI Moves the "Decision Visibility Horizon" Further into the Future.

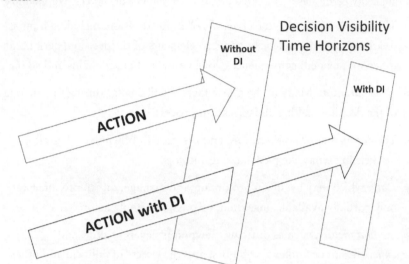

Key Insight #22: Many decisions made by large organizations, and society as a whole, have reached a level of complexity that has outgrown the capabilities of informal decision making processes. The stakes have become too high, and the game is now played too fast for relying on intuition and luck alone. We need a system that gives us the best chance of winning.

The complexity that limits the effectiveness of decision makers comes in many guises and crosses many industries. One classic dilemma is the seemingly irreconcilable separation between data-driven, "analytic" approaches to supporting decisions, vs "inductive," intuitive approaches. Both have their own strengths and limitations, but rarely are the two harnessed to cooperate within a unified decision making framework. Generally, they compete, with justifications based on "gut reactions" regarded, at least from a methodological standpoint, as at odds with "rational" analysis. In fact, this dichotomy is not only artificial, but often is detrimental to decision outcomes.

Dimensions of Complexity

Complexity permeates decision making from a number of sources. For example:

- The *number of factors to be considered* in the decision, including inputs, desired results, dependencies between elements of the decision, peripheral (often unintended) consequences, long cause-and-effect chains and so on.

- *Time variation*. Many of the above factors will change during the lifetime of the decision making and execution process.

- The *dominance of nonlinearities* and the growth of winner-takes-all markets in arenas like media and technology.

- *Data*, which may be difficult to obtain and manage, difficult to interpret, only partially available, uncertain, or possibly simply incorrect.

- *Human factors*, such as differing viewpoints, levels of skills and experience of decision contributors, and the effects of political and other social relationships.

How *Not* to Handle Complexity

Common responses to these challenges include gathering more data, hiring experts (statisticians, modelers, and others), building more complex statistical models, or placing greater demands on IT — often in the form of building an information architecture that allows greater sharing and collaboration.

Although these approaches may sometimes be helpful, they are often not enough and fail to address the root of the problem. They lack integration between the facts and figures used to make choices, human expert judgment, and the technology platform, if any. In many organizations, systems, data, and human stakeholders are separated by culture, language, geographical distance, and time delays.

Taking these steps is like hiring new experts to build your building, while still lacking a blueprint.

The Complexity Ceiling Leads to Unintended Consequences

For now, though, let's go back to that trip to the European company with the hot-air balloons.

The core problem we solved for our client was to help them to understand — through a structured diagram and process — how decisions cross through multiple organizations. Understanding this *internal* complexity was challenging enough, but we hope we helped them on their way toward understanding *external* complexities as well, such as the ones that the climate change activists were protesting. Without DI or something like it, we have found time and again that organizations are lost in complexity. Large transnationals like our client are particularly prone to systemic risk from outside their organizations, and so a systems understanding is no longer a luxury, but a necessity and fiscal responsibility to stakeholders.

Yet despite these new challenges, the way that we work together to make complex decisions has remained unchanged. New product launches are still decided in the board room. Commercial loans are still underwritten without an understanding of the complexities of corporate ownership. Entire divisions and initiatives are launched — and disbanded — without a rigorous analysis process. Legislation is enacted without careful impact analysis and tracking.

Why? Because, despite massive amounts of new data, our tools haven't kept up.

> **Key Insight #23:** We have reached a *complexity ceiling*: a point where the challenges facing us in many areas are unmatched by the tools available to address them, and so systematic biases and thinking flaws lead to unintended consequences. (A search in the Google Ngram database shows a considerable increase in the appearance of the phrase 'unintended consequences' from 1940 through 2000 [41].)

And there's a gap between data and decisions which means that we have — with apologies to Colerige — "heaps and heaps of data, but none that help us think."

BORROWING FROM ENGINEERING:
SOLUTIONS TO COMPLEXITY

DI is emerging simultaneously in many areas worldwide because it follows a historical pattern: From the first flint axe through the great pyramids, and on to skyscrapers and rocket ships, we have learned to work collaboratively to solve problems and create complex artifacts that could never be made by one person working alone.

In the progression of each of these technologies, there has come a point where our ability to create reaches its limit. This is the *complexity ceiling*: beyond which we can't progress without a new approach. And today – as in other times before the solution becomes widely known – there is a period of widespread breakdown: bridges collapse, cars crash, and buildings catch on fire. Or, as today, we are challenged on many fronts including poverty, inequality, democracy, and climate.

These problems create a shared sense of pressure to discover solutions. And throughout history, the solutions have these common elements:

- A *formal visual language* that removed ambiguity and facilitated information and knowledge-sharing and alignment among groups with widely different skills and backgrounds (for instance, a set of computer-assisted design primitives (shapes) that are used to create an electrical motor).

- A *design* discipline that guides how to create the visual picture, including best practices and typical mistakes to be avoided (for instance, the design skills needed to create a good blueprint).

- A system for *tasks* that are used by different kinds of experts to work together (for instance, creating an electrical design for a building).

- Defined *quality control* checks and balances for each set of tasks (for instance, a review process that a diverse team can use to check that software is defect-free before it is released to the public).

Together, these are the elements that make up an engineering discipline. And so we learned that:

> **Key Insight #24:** Decision making is an *engineering* discipline, and a CDD is an *artifact* that can be managed like many other designed and engineered objects.

So DI includes these elements, which derive from engineering best practices [42]:

- Recognition that the decision making process follows a *lifecycle* beginning with the formulation of the problem and ending with the completion of the solution.

- Clear definition of decision *requirements* and translation of these into a specification that everyone agrees to for the decision to be made.

- An *iterative design process* that incorporates data and expert judgment, allows for multiple data scenarios, and models different potential worlds. The design process produces the CDD and related documentation.

- *Quality assurance* (QA) and *security* steps at each stage. Decision QA comprises processes that detect potential errors in a decision. We can evaluate a decision for incorrect assumptions, flawed reasoning, statistical bias, and other errors. Also key to quality is ensuring that uncertainties in the data used to support the decision are clearly identified and that the effect of these uncertainties, as they propagate through the decision model to the outputs, is clearly understood.

  Says Informed Decisions CTO Håkan Edvinsson:

  > *my DI model QA activity helps me and my stakeholders to gain trust in the model and in the DI method. I do it by back-testing: using historical data and running a decision forward to obtain the outcome that actually happened [43].*

- Clear "hooks" that identify where intelligence technologies (such as those shown in Figure 26) connect into the general framework.

- The core to the implementation phase is decision *execution*, which in all but the simplest of environments must be tightly coupled with *monitoring key assumptions* to ensure that they remain inside the bounds within which the decision model yields the desired outcomes.

- As a decision is implemented in an organization, *alignment* is critical. This includes ensuring that the decision — including basics like agreement on definitions of key terminology — are consistently understood.

  As decisions change in response to a dynamic environment, more diligent alignment practices become especially important. An organization that requires months to communicate a change in strategic direction to its employees loses agility. Alignment is assisted by a number of DI best practices, especially the CDD, which helps to communicate the decision and its rationale as the decision planning process evolves, and as the environment changes during the implementation lifetime of the decision.

Note that dashboards and revenue assurance techniques fit here: instead of monitoring arbitrarily, we do so in the context of planning expectations. If, during monitoring, new information arises indicating the original decision should be adjusted, then decision planning activities are restarted.

The above phases provide a structure for organizing decision engineering best practices. Although many existing practices within organizations today fit into various parts of this framework, until now they have not been integrated into a single process, nor have they been recognized as constituting an engineering discipline. By unifying them into this framework, we not only have a rigorous approach to planning decisions, maximizing both the quantitative data and the human expertise at hand, but a means for utilizing the products of the planning phase to help guide execution of the decision, most particularly, to deal with change over time. Furthermore, by recognizing the methodology specifically as an engineering discipline, we find many opportunities to validate, improve, and extend it by comparing it with other engineering disciplines, many of which have aspects of their histories that closely parallel decision engineering.

Perhaps, most importantly, DI creates, for the first time, a standardized conceptual framework, with an associated set of processes, to improve the success rates of complex decisions and their implementation. The framework enables decision makers to overcome the complexity of the situations they face, within the timelines available to them, by using analytic techniques that have a long, proven history in other disciplines.

Furthermore, the documentation produced during decision-planning provides a rich shared base for future decisions. Unlike traditional "decision support" materials, which are normally ad hoc and rarely find ongoing use after the decision is made[2], CDDs have a well-defined structure and become an integral part of the implementation process. Because they remain as "living" documents and are often reused, CDDs naturally encode "lessons from history" into an organization's decision making culture.

DECISION INTELLIGENCE BRIDGES FROM AI/ML THEORY TO PRACTICE

As I introduced above, one way to view DI is as a technology that bridges the gap between Artificial Intelligence theory to practice. DI uses AI, data, human expertise, and other technologies to support organizations as they reason through complex cause-and-effect chains from policies and actions to business outcomes. These chains can include "soft" cause-and-effect links as well as traditional financial ones.

For example, a DI model can help a team to analyze how, although an investment in hiring disabled people may be more costly in the short run, it produces substantial value in the long run, through reduced attrition, increased productivity, and the high morale and motivation that comes to a workforce that is driven by an increased sense of compassion [44] [2].

> **Key Insight #25:** DI can be thought of as the next natural extension of artificial intelligence: it fills important gaps in how we currently use AI and ML.

Indeed, Google's Cassie Kozyrkov calls Decision Intelligence "Machine Learning ++" [45].

A secondary benefit of DI is that it allows more complex situations (such as the justification for a business investment) to be understood, and the assumptions upon which they depend made explicit, validated, and tracked as they change over time. Following this example, for organizations to fully appreciate the value of disability hiring, they must:

- Understand *soft factors* internal to the business which lead to improved financial performance, as above.

- Model the *"triple bottom line"* including financial, social, and environmental impacts. Frank Spencer of Kedge calls these "simultaneous multiples."

- Model *externalities*, to understand how the organization's impact on its larger competitive, social, environmental, and market environment creates "boomerang" effects that can benefit that organization in the long run. This is in contrast to many traditional companies that operate by assuming infinite sources and sinks. This limited thinking is causing considerable social and environmental negative impacts. DI empowers organizations with the tools to embrace proactive modeling of these factors.

- Be able to find the "sweet spot" between profit and purpose: where both financial and social goals can be met simultaneously.

> **Key Insight #26:** Sophisticated DI tools can find "holy grails": those rare and priceless solutions that satisfy all parties in an otherwise contentious situation.

Consider, in particular, how an organization might determine the cost/benefit impact of the specialized training required to hire and employ an employee prospect with autism. The organization might want to see how much it would cost to train a candidate and then to project the productivity impact or other benefit it could expect to obtain.

This organization might use DI to build a model that captures assumptions and metrics such as the dollar cost of an hour of training, the current and target skill level of a candidate or group of candidates and the expected number of hours required to achieve the target skill level. Once it has built the initial model, the organization can test various scenarios by changing investment levels, costs, operational variables, and/or desired outcomes.

For example, based on institutional experience, the organization might add to the model the expected cost of missing a project's deadlines. The various scenarios can be adjusted collaboratively in real time and the results represented visually. See, for example, this interactive DI model that shows how to think about a training program [39]; and this one, illustrated in Figure 28, which helps an organization to think about the dynamics of its

Figure 28. An Interactive Carbon Tax Emissions Decision Model.

investment in a system that reduces carbon emissions [46] (follow the link in the bibliography to try this model yourself now).

The Democratization Power of Simplicity

One way to look at DI is that it places a layer of usability on top of these powerful technologies.

Since the goal of DI is to bring complex technologies into the board room, legislature, and other situations that have proven not ready to embrace detailed mathematics or algorithms, this usability layer is essential.

This is why these technologies all must relate to the CDD or something like it, which is natural and low-friction, minimizing the mental effort required to understand it. It is unrealistic to expect these leaders to learn a new methodology like predicate logic or causal inference notation. Otherwise, all but the most dedicated will return to "decision by PowerPoint" or, more dangerously, "decision by the strongest personality in the room."

THE RIGHT DECISION IN A CHANGING CONTEXT

No sensible decision can be made any longer without taking into account not only the world as it is, but the world as it will be.
— Isaac Asimov [47]

The outcome from a decision doesn't just change based on your actions. It also depends on the *context*: circumstances that are outside of your control that answer the question:

What is the situation now, and in the future, and what can I do now in order to interact with that external situation in order to achieve the outcomes that I want?

And then as the external situation changes, and perhaps changes in a way that I didn't expect, how can I go back and modify that decision to keep ensuring I keep achieving my outcome?

Like never before, global decisions are no longer made in a static environment. Instead, we're navigating through a continuously incoming

Figure 29. The Outcomes from Your Decisions Depend on the Actions You Take as well as the External Circumstances You Can't Change, or the *Context*.

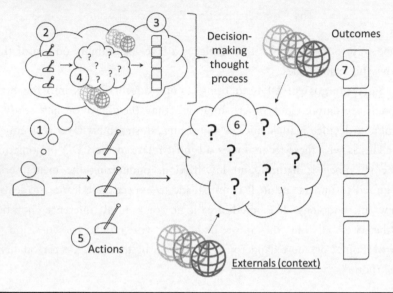

flux of information as it impinges upon us through time. Figure 29 shows where these external factors fit into the framework. As you can see, this is a lot to keep track of mentally, so computer help to combine these factors can make a big difference.

Chapter 3 now describes the technologies that are integrating into the DI framework, along with how they fit into the CDD archetype. Chapter 4 then gets practical, taking you through a number of decision model examples.

NOTES

1. This name, as with all of those in examples here, has been anonymized.

2. We have met senior leaders of several projects – in governments and industry – with budgets in the tens of millions of dollars who express frustration at having to "start from scratch" because the decision rationale of their predecessors was not recorded in a way that it could be reused.

CHAPTER 3

TECHNOLOGIES, DISCIPLINES, AND OTHER PUZZLE PIECES OF THE SOLUTIONS RENAISSANCE

For generations, we have rewarded deep knowledge of individual disciplines, such as chemistry, economics, technology, physics, etc. while not paying the attention necessary to unify these solutions when required to address much larger problems.

— John McMullen [48]

Wisdom is the intelligence of the system as a whole.

— Gregory Bateson [49]

THE WEB OF WICKED PROBLEMS

Since the Renaissance, civilization has developed a cornucopia of specialist disciplines. Today, we have reached a moment in time where we are challenged to reconnect them to solve the hardest problems facing the human race: democracy, climate, conflict, and more. (Some call these "wicked problems" [50].) A common pattern underlies these outstanding unsolved problems: they are only solved through an integrated approach — try to solve conflict without addressing the economy, and you will fail. Try to solve democracy without addressing the status of women worldwide, for instance, and you will fail.

Indeed, the Millennium Project identifies these challenges as an interdependent web, as shown in Figure 30.

Figure 30. The Millennium Project's 15 Global Challenges.

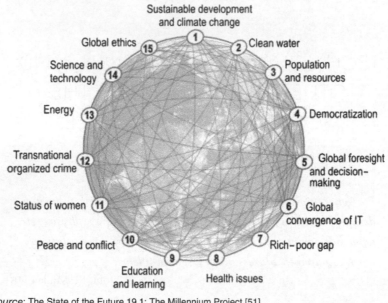

Source: The State of the Future 19.1; The Millennium Project [51].

The Millennium Project's challenge #5 is, in essence, the goal of Decision Intelligence (DI):

> *Decisionmakers are rarely trained in foresight and decisionmaking, even though decision support and foresight systems are constantly being improved with artificial intelligence, big data analytics, simulations, collective intelligence systems, e-governance participatory systems, and a deeper understanding of psychological factors that impinge on decisionmaking and its outcomes [...] and as mobile apps proliferate. [52]*

DI addresses this limitation in multiple ways. At its most basic level, it provides a standard way of drawing the picture of decision impacts as they bounce between arenas like those shown earlier. This is the causal decision diagram (CDD). As introduced earlier, the CDD is a framework into which these technologies and disciplines fit.

This chapter describes many of the key technologies and disciplines of the Solutions Renaissance, connecting them back to DI and the CDD. Note that each one is the topic of many books, and sometimes entire journals and academic departments. For this reason, my treatment is by necessity cursory, with the goal of giving you a taste of each one and how it fits into the DI framework.

BIG DATA

Big data is just a big rear-view mirror, not the clear windshield that IT vendors pretend. It tells us nothing about the future.
— Milo Jones and Philippe Silberzahn [53]

Data is, in many ways, the "seventh sense" of humanity. Data from the Mars Rover tell us about the surface of the planet, and data from Voyager tell us about the outer reaches of the solar system. Closer to home, marketing companies like Google now own massive amounts of data on human behavior [54, 55], and health companies like Fitbit have discovered information about sleeping and fitness trends based on hundreds of thousands of individuals, far more than the largest scientific study [56–58].

The US National Oceanic and Atmospheric Administration (NOAA) publishes petabytes (that's over a thousand terabytes, each of which is over a thousand gigabytes) of data.

NOAA has 10s of petabytes of data stored in various ways, and produces more than 15 million products daily — from weather forecasts for New York City to tide-gauge observations in Seattle — which it said amounts to about 20 terabytes per day. This is twice the data of the entire printed collection of the U.S. Library of Congress. [59]

McKinsey says 30 billion pieces of content are saved on Facebook every month [60] and that US health care data will be worth US $300 billion [61]. USAID's Spatial Data Repository [58] is a trove of map-based spatial data. The RECAP project [62] publishes US court opinions going back for centuries.

However,

Key Insight #27: The tsunami of data is matched by a desert of systems that can make good use of that data.

According to the TM Forum, for instance, there is a "growing gulf between companies' desire to embrace Big Data and their ability to operationalize it […]," and knowledge and best practices about how to translate data into value are sorely lacking [63].

Underlying the inadequate use of data is the fact that using it for predictions and decisions requires a fundamentally new way of managing, cleansing, and thinking about it. I encounter data myths every day in my work. Basic myths like "the model is only as good as the data" persist. And few organizations recognize that some data have far more predictive power than others. This has been a boon to my own work, where companies recognize our team's ability to refine data "raw material" into Artificial Intelligence (AI) and DI systems that generate business value. Yet our projects are only a drop in a bucket and represent only the beginning of many years of future value.

So, even though systems that store and process Big Data are essential technical contributors to DI, they are realizing only a fraction of their value today due to many systematic misunderstandings and missed opportunities. These include the following:

- *Many systems today are built to capture data about the present and the past, but haven't been mined to understand cause-and-effect links that could help support decisions about the future.* For instance, your local utility stores information about your monthly electrical usage, but it probably hasn't yet used that data to discover how to predict which customers would be most interested in an app that allowed them to save energy by controlling their thermostat while away from home and was, at the same time, respectful of protecting their private information. Your local city government probably maintains good data about traffic patterns but hasn't used them to decide where to create bike lanes to reduce city greenhouse gas emissions and congestion in your city.

  Key Insight #28: The most important untapped type of data storage is not facts and figures, but cause-and-effect links: relationships that connect one event to another.

- *Though 10% of the fields in a database usually have 90% of its predictive power,* few organizations know how to determine which fields those are. Without this kind of insight, many companies and governments spend months or years cleaning all their data instead of some of it, at what can amount to massive unnecessary cost.

Key Insight #29: All data are not equal; it is a monumental waste of time to manage the less-valuable data fields.

- *Small data has value too.* Some cause-and-effect patterns in data are so strong they can be found easily, in a few fields and, without a lot of examples, in dirty data. Yet our focus on Big Data means we often overlook this fact.

Key Insight #30: What matters is not the number of rows or columns in your data set, but the strength of its signal relative to noise.

- *There is a disproportionate focus on using data for prediction instead of decisions.* Microsoft, for example, described part of its Big Data strategy as follows:

We demonstrated [...] where we took historical meteorological data over decades and historical airline flight-delay data over decades and we built a predictive model that combined them. We could then ask, "On a clear day, what are the probabilities of delay for various airlines, airports and times?" Based on the historical meteorological data, we could also ask, "What do those probabilities look like when there's six inches of snow in Detroit?" [64]

But such a prediction has no value unless it ultimately leads to an action. What matters is not an answer to (for instance): "what are the chances I'll miss my connection?", but rather "what flight should I book to (1) maximize my chances of making it; (2) make it most likely I can fly on a 787; (3) minimize my miles in the air; and (4) avoid Detroit if at all possible?" We need to be asking the *decision* questions, and connecting all of the dots to include outcomes through a complete causal chain.

Relative to the CDD, data have several roles:

- As a source of information about *externals*: those factors that are outside of our control, but which interact with our decisions to lead to outcomes. There are two primary forms of externals:
  - those which are unchanging over the time period of the decision model, such as the diameter of the earth; and

  - predictions about things we cannot change, such as the predicted rainfall for the next 12 months.

- As a source of training data from which to determine how each link operates. This can include:
  - training data for a machine learning (ML) model;

  - data to be used to build a statistic that captures an important causation or correlation;

  - data from a randomized control trial (RCT);

  - data to inform another kind of model, like an agent-based, game theory, analytic hierarchy process (AHP), or other; and

  - qualitative data that help to inform "soft" links.

Note that data may come from inside or outside our organization. As decision modeling becomes more sophisticated, our ability to model the complex dynamics at play as our organization interacts with the outside world, and vice versa, becomes more practical.

The aforementioned list is not exhaustive. More details about several of these uses of data are described below.

WARM DATA

Systems pioneer Nora Bateson heads the global International Bateson Institute and is Gregory Bateson's daughter.

In the early 2010s, she attended a presentation showing data regarding troop movements in Syria. Bateson observed that the presentation – along with the decisions described – omitted important contextual information from a number of realms: what was the local attitude toward the warfighters? What would be the economic impact of an invasion? What were the geopolitical implications of this battle on the proxy war of which it was a part? So she challenged the audience: "Where is the warm data—the data about these relationships and connections?" [65].

Today, Bateson offers warm data workshops worldwide. Their goal is to convey the importance of data that capture these relationships – the *Link* in this book's title. She explains:

> *This is different than action or qualitative research. It is about the relationships between the stakeholders. You can have all the data in the world on them, but unless you study their relationships, you are missing a critical dimension.*

Regarding causal chains, Bateson [66] says that:

> *Causation is like soup: humans have multiple contextual infusions that they consolidate simultaneously to make decisions. Upon first meeting a person, for instance, we don't think of one thing at a time: you take in specific words they're using, the level at which they speak, you make judgments about their background and way of speaking, there is a deeper resonance of material that is cross referencing and cross contextualizing as two people are sense-making together. This process is not necessarily accessible to conscious thought.*

Bateson goes on to explain that this pattern repeats in other realms, from individual human trauma to families, to organizations, and ecology. Change, she says, happens at a system level. A tree, for instance, is "in a state of mutual responsiveness calibration with all the other organisms: it is creating shade and responding to shade. It is creating obstructions to wind and responding to wind [66]." We ignore these relationships at our peril. To represent, understand, and modify these kinds of systems, therefore, Bateson's team needed a new way to think about data, to represent relational transcontextual information, which is what she calls warm data today: moving past a "monochromatic tonality" of data to a greater spectrum of representational richness.

Warm data gives perspective on double binds, paradoxes, contradictions, and the movements of complex systems. It also acknowledges the importance of the *esthetic* – the felt-body or somatic sense of "wrongness" or "rightness" that is one way our unconscious communicates its insights. The International Bateson Institute's warm data workshops help participants appreciate the richness of these interdependent relationships, along with classic mistakes that arise when they are ignored, and best practices for managing it.

Bateson cautions against the overuse of diagrams like CDDs. She says that they can gain too much authority, that we can tell ourselves, "yes, we can use these blueprints, and we know it's not enough [66]," but that we can subsequently lose perspective: "the second the blueprint comes into the room it has authority" which may lead to the suppression of diverse ideas or − worse − the use of these diagrams for persuasion instead of illumination and alignment. This points out an unintended consequence of CDDs, which I believe can be mitigated by awareness and by methods that convene meetings that allow them to be, as Bateson explains, "held loosely" so as to fit changing contextual circumstances.

ARTIFICIAL INTELLIGENCE AND MACHINE LEARNING

I showed how ML fits into CDDs in Chapter 2. This section describes how a ML model is created.

Let's say you want to build a new app that translates the language of dogs to English. The basic idea is you point your mobile phone at your dog and it translates what your dog is communicating: "I am hungry" or "I am feeling anxious." Hundreds of thousands of pets are euthanized today because their owners don't understand them, and can't help them. Such an app would be groundbreaking, connecting humans to the natural world in a way that would have far-reaching consequences. (Indeed, as I write these words, I'm honored to be part of an early-stage team making exactly this happen [66].)

Or imagine you are a city manager, and you want to know how much an investment in a public awareness campaign about littering might reduce trash in the streets ... and then how much that reduced trash would decrease crime.

Both of these software apps can be built today because of ML: an important subfield within the larger field of AI. These fields sound intimidating and complex, but so does the technology behind a microwave oven, and yet many of us use them every day to cook. Just as I can teach a child to use a microwave ("open the door," "put in your food"), you can learn the basics of AI [45]. Indeed, as AI systems become more and more pervasive − driving everything from Google advertising to fake news that targets you to influence your vote — arming yourself with an understanding of this technology is critical. In the not-so-distant future, you'll be able to create AIs of your own that assist you with many of the tasks the internet is trying to manipulate you into performing: from purchasing a new car, to choosing who to vote for, to deciding what college to attend or what company to acquire. This "AI for everyone" movement is just getting started.

In addition, an "outside of the box" (open the microwave door ... then put in your food ... and so on) understanding of AI is critical to the unified DI mission that is the core of this book (recall I introduced the inside/outside-of-the-box distinction in Chapter 1). I promise you, experts on economics, sociology, complex systems, and all the other technologies mentioned in this book will never understand the internals of AI systems. Yet they can *use* them effectively as part of an overall DI infrastructure that solves wicked problems. The good news is that "outside of the AI box" is quite easy to understand.

The rest of this section provides this understanding.

AI History: Winters and Summers

The AI market is expected to grow at a rapid rate to US $1.2 trillion worldwide [67] fueled by initiatives like The US Defense Advanced Research Projects Agency (DARPA)'s US $2 billion "AI Next" initiative and US $1 trillion investment expected by China alone by 2030 [68]. AI is considered a fast-growing and important technology. Bill Gates said that "If you invent a breakthrough in artificial intelligence, so machines can learn [...] that is worth 10 Microsofts" [69]. Former President Barack Obama observed that "AI [...] promises to create a vastly more productive and efficient economy" [70].

AI is well on the road to mass adoption [71], for better or worse.

This success comes after about a half-century of effort, during which time the field has gone through two "AI winter" periods: following "hot" periods in the 1970s and 1980s, AI's substance didn't match its hype. Despite a few notable AI successes during the subsequent "winters" (AI has been used for decades in breast cancer screening and in credit card fraud detection), it took until around 2010 for the technology to advance sufficiently to garner the kind of well-justified quotes as those above, from Bill Gates and others [71].

During this long gestation, the field of AI went through a number of changes. Early efforts were focused on systems that used logic to capture intelligence. The core elements here were rules and facts like "All elephants are gray" and "Harold is an elephant" that led to conclusions like "Harold is gray."

A second camp received less attention until recently, yet has been the most successful to date. Called "subsymbolic" AI, the idea was to use a simplified model of a brain cell — a neuron — as the fundamental element from which AI systems were to be built. Most AI systems today use this model, and most of them are ML systems, as described below.

Understanding the Core of AI

ML is a way to build computer programs that learn from examples. Instead of writing software, ML practitioners like myself (and like you, sooner than you think) "teach" the computer using tables of data that give it examples of the kinds of inputs we want it to process, and the "right answer" for each example.

Figure 31 shows a simple example, where we want to predict whether a bird is likely to eat fish based on its bodily features. As can be seen in the figure, every row of the table contains two parts, *inputs* and *targets*. Inputs include a list of features of birds: 4″ bill, 10″ legs, brown head, 3″ toes, white eyes, and so forth. Targets are whether that bird eats fish or not: "yes" or "no" for each row of data.

ML software takes a table like Figure 31 as the input and produces a learned *model* that captures the pattern shown in the data (in this case, the

Figure 31. Simple Machine Learning Training Data Example.

	Gazintas				Gazouta
Bill length	Leg length	Head color	Toe length	Eye color	Eats fish?
4	3	white	1.5	brown	Y
2	1	green	4	red	N
...(and so forth)					

Now, here's the best part:

Figure 32. Schematic for How Most Machine Learning/AI Systems Work Today.

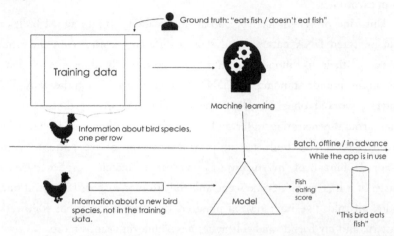

pattern that links the characteristics of a bird to the likelihood of whether it eats fish or not). The model is the artificial "brain" of a ML system.

The general pattern shown in Figure 32 underlies the vast majority of ML systems in use today. Amazon chooses which books to recommend to you based on a score produced by a model trained on book sales. Facebook identifies the location of your face in an image based on position scores that use training data consisting of images where humans have labeled the faces. (In this kind of system, each row in the training data schematic shown in Figure 31 corresponds to an image in which the faces have been labeled.) Credit card fraud systems use training data from historical fraud and non-fraud situations to produce a score reflecting the likelihood that a particular transaction is fraudulent.

> **Key Insight #31:** It's easy to understand the "outside of the box" in ML systems: you create a set of training data, where each row is an example of the input and output. This is used to build a model, which is used to mimic the prediction shown in the training data.

Inside the box, the machine is recognizing patterns. So, in the example in Figure 31, the learner might realize that if the legs are over a foot long, and the bill is over three inches long, the bird always eats fish. It builds this relationship into the model. Typical ML models are built from thousands of columns in the training data (*features*): too many for humans to find the subtle patterns within them that distinguish the different kinds of target fields from each other.[1]

This kind of system has very broad applicability. Years ago, I built one that analyzed DNA patterns and scored different positions on the strand based on their likelihood to contain a ribosomal binding site (which is important in understanding how DNA produces structures in the body) [72]. Later, I worked on a US Department of Energy project that used data from ground-penetrating radar and other sensors to find buried hazardous waste [73]. I have built systems that follow the above pattern for the Colorado Bureau of Investigation to produce a "match score" between an image of a hair from a crime scene and that from a suspect [74]. And much more: all told, I've built several hundred different models that follow this pattern, and my friends and colleagues have built thousands more.

Not only does ML make building software to solve complex problems much easier (essentially, the computer programs itself by looking at examples), it can also solve previously unsolvable problems like face recognition and book recommendation. This is because of the ability of the computer to do what humans cannot: finding subtle patterns that humans are incapable of detecting among millions or billons of examples (rows in the training data).

Beyond Supervised Learning: AI's Bigger Picture

AI does go beyond the pattern that is shown in Figure 32, which I estimate accounts for about 80% of the deployed applications today. The architecture shown there is called *supervised learning* because the target field (also called the *ground truth*) is like a "supervisor" telling the system what to say for each row of the data.

> **Key Insight #32:** If you want to understand the most widely used form of AI today, focus on supervised learning.

Other types of AI are as follows:

- *Natural language processing (NLP).* AI systems that can understand text are an important and growing subfield. I predict that NLP will be as important as supervised learning within the next 12–18 months.

The most widespread NLP models do *text classification* and *text matching*. Text classification systems take a block of text and scores it to reflect how well it represents a particular category. For instance, a model might take a Twitter tweet as input and produce a "happiness score," or take a Facebook post as input and produce an "interested in buying something" score.

For an example of text matching, a system might take as input a person's resume and produce a score indicating its match to a job description.

Given that the amount of online text produced today is exploding, these applications are becoming more and more important, and will likely explode in usage as much as supervised learning has done today.

- *Unsupervised learning.* Here, there is no target column field in the training data: the system only receives the input side of the table. The model that it produces is used for one of two purposes: (1) as input to a later supervised learning process (sometimes it's expensive to obtain ground truth, so this pre-training can be helpful) or (2) to detect the degree to which an input to the model is an *anomaly*: different from any of the samples shown in the training data.

- *Expert systems.* These are software systems that capture the expertise within some profession, whether it involves diagnosing a disease or selling to telecoms. They are based on logic, which is used to represent that expertise. Expert systems were the driver of the mid-1980s AI hype cycle and were at the core of Japan's US$850 million Fifth Generation investment in AI [75], the US $100 million per year for 20 years Cyc project [76, 77], and the UK's £350 million investment in the Alvey project [78].

- *Reinforcement learning (RL) systems.* The newest class of AI systems making the leap from research to applications is RL algorithms, RL uses software agents that take actions in an environment and seek to maximize some measurement of a reward over time. For instance, DI company Prowler.io uses RL for logistics management: it creates multiple models of possible futures, each with a different demand for resources.

    For Prowler, agent jobs might be to act as a pick-up truck, a delivery truck, a taxi, or a shared-ride system like Lyft. The RL system conducts a simulation during which the agents learn from their experience through success and failure with their tasks. RL is the method by which an agent changes its behavior policy to make it more likely to be successful on each subsequent simulation run [79].

AI in Context

I am often asked "what's the difference between AI, machine learning, and deep learning? And what about the robot apocalypse?" Figure 33 summarizes my answer.

Working from the outside in, "strong" AI is also known as "artificial general intelligence" and is reflected by such movie characters as Hal from *2001: A Space Odyssey* and the AI love interest in the movie *Her*. Although strong AI is good for science fiction, most professional AI researchers agree that it is a long way off.

Figure 33. The Relationship between Various Types of AI.

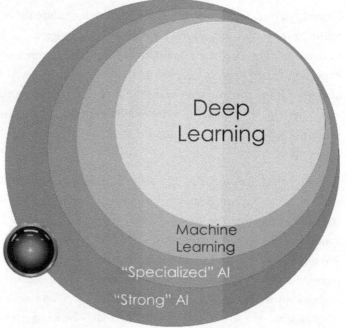

Key Insight #33: The danger of strong AI, or AGI, is the distraction it represents from the important, hard problems that AI can help us to solve today, by working hand-in-hand with human experts.

Most AI today is "specialized," meaning that it solves some specific problem. Most of those systems are ML solutions, the most successful of which are deep learning methods, which constitute the majority of deployed systems today. There are ML techniques that are not deep learning – one that I particularly like is decision tree learning methods like CART [80] – and there are AI systems that are not learning systems, such as many NLP systems.

Decision Models Are NOT Decision Trees

Some people confuse CDDs with another technology called a "decision tree" [81], which is a diagram or model that tells you the right decision to make in a range of situations/scenarios. It steps through external factors and indicates the best decision for multiple combinations of factors.

For example, a decision tree might explain how to diagnose a patient. First, measure their blood pressure. Then, if it is high, do a blood test. If it is low, do a tilt table test, and so forth. A decision tree is a compact representation of how to go about finding an answer to a question, such as "what illness does this patient have?"

A decision model helps you to determine the best actions in multiple scenarios. A decision tree documents what those actions are.

Another way to use a decision tree is to use a decision tree *learning* method: these take training data table just like the one above as input and produces a model as output. The model, once built, takes input data and produce predictions or labels. So the input and output to decision tree learning is the same as for deep learning. The difference is that accuracy is not as high for some problems. The huge advantage is that a decision tree learner is much easier to understand.

CAUSAL REASONING

Logic is a poor model of cause and effect.

– Gregory Bateson [49]

One of the reasons DI is a new field traces back to a strange gap in the history of science. We know, of course, that closing the door of a car does not cause it to pull out of the garage. And we also know that pushing the gas pedal after placing the car in reverse *does* have such a causative effect. Yet until recently, science has lacked a formal notation for distinguishing things like the first example, in which actions or events frequently occur together – *correlations* – from those like the second example, in which there is a *causal* relationship. Causal relationships are the justification for the creation of links in a CDD.

In his breakthrough 2018 book, *The Book of Why*, Turing Award winner Judea Pearl introduces a new scientific formulation for causal reasoning to a broad audience [23]. An AI expert, Pearl is on a similar track to DI in his recognition that the lack of multi-link causal structures in current AI systems represents their most fundamental limitation.

Simply put, causal reasoning is about understanding what things cause other things in the world to happen together. This is easy enough for causations we directly observe every day, like that gas pedal. It is harder to understand when the evidence for causation is buried in a big data set. If two things tend to happen, but not apart, is one causing the other? How can we use data to distinguish the door slamming, which is not causative, from the gas pedal, which is? And once we have made this determination, how can we capture that knowledge in such a way that we don't lose the distinction?

Answering questions like these is outside the scope of this book, because we can go a long way toward building CDDs without knowing this theory. Simply drawing good collaborative pictures of our "common sense" understanding of causation is such a great step forward that we shouldn't allow formal theories of causation to get in the way. This can be dangerous, though; so an important direction for DI is to translate formal causation theory into a form that can be used for nontechnical practitioners.

In the meantime, we can get a long way by asking, for each link in a CDD, whether it is really a cause or might be just a correlation (in which case we usually want to spend some time looking upstream to find the cause that led to both correlating factors). If, for example, we observe that people who eat breakfast are, in general, healthier, then we might conclude that breakfast eating causes this greater health, as shown in the left-hand side of Figure 34. It may, however, be true that health-conscious people engage in both behaviors, which is another explanation for the same observation, shown on the right-hand side of Figure 34.

Figure 34. Two Causative Explanations for Why People Who Eat Breakfast Are Healthier.

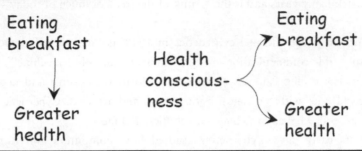

Causal reasoning is broader than DI, because it deals with causal pathways (like those including cancer cells [82] or nuclear reactors) that do not start with a decision and lead to an outcome. Moving forward, DI and causal reasoning will interact substantially, as causal reasoning provides mechanisms for building better DI models, and DI helps to democratize causal reasoning so it can be used by non-expert decision makers.

As quoted in the *New York Times*, Facebook Chief AI Scientist Yann LeCun agrees that causal reasoning is an important element in the future of AI, along with supporting decision making. As described there, the four abilities that help us navigate the world are:

(1) perception and categorization of the world around us;

(2) contextualization of the relationships between things;

(3) prediction to understand cause and effect; and

(4) planning and decision making based on external and internal factors.

The article says that AI meets or exceeds human performance in (1), above, and that it is not yet near human performance in (2) through (4). These next three phases are, without coincidence, pillars of DI [83].

CYBERNETICS

Despite its deep connections to DI, the field of cybernetics has been largely "off the map" for AI and DI practitioners: it was never mentioned to me in the seven years of my masters and PhD in AI. Yet cybernetics is probably the closest field to the theme of this book and, despite being ignored by many, it goes back many years and is the "trunk of the tree" of much of today's high tech.

Norbert Wiener defined cybernetics in 1948 as "the scientific study of control and communication in the animal and the machine" [84]. Cybernetics studies causal systems, with a focus on positive and negative feedback loops within systems, both natural and artificial. Cybernetic concepts are today baked in to biology, robotics, and more.

In its early days, cybernetics studied how computers and humans interact, and led to the fields of human−computer interaction (HCI) and ergonomics [85]. It was AI before AI had its name.

Cognitive science also owes its ancestry to cybernetics, as does modern neural-network-based ML, with early papers such as 1943's Warren McCulloch and Walter Pitts' "A Logical Calculus of the Ideas Immanent in Nervous Activity" [86].

Today, the "cyber" prefix lives on robustly in popular culture. And the UK's Cybernetics Society celebrated its 50th anniversary in 2018 [87]. Despite its DNA in many modern disciplines, however, the field itself has not fared as well [88]. Peter Asaro says that:

> Cybernetics slowly dissolved as a coherent scientific field during the 1970s, though its influence is still broadly felt. Cybernetic concepts and theories continue on, reconstituted in various guises, including the fields of self-organizing systems, dynamical systems, complex/chaotic/non-linear systems, communications theory, operations research, cognitive science, Artificial Intelligence, artificial life, Robotics, Human-Computer Interaction, multi-agent systems and artificial neural networks. [89]

From this point of view, *Link* can be thought of as one of the several efforts to re-cohere the cybernetic diaspora.

COMPLEX SYSTEMS/COMPLEXITY THEORY/COMPLEXITY SCIENCE

Previous sections described causal modeling, systems dynamics, systems thinking, and warm data. Complex systems are closely related to these concepts, and have considerable overlap. As a rule, a system is considered *complex* if it is difficult to calculate what the system will do without running a simulation. Complex systems exhibit behaviors like self-organization, non-linearity, feedback loops, self-organization, and emergence. Complex systems can be found in many fields, from social networking on the internet to economics, to the interactions of trees in a forest.

Complexity Expert Dave Snowden distinguishes complex situations from chaotic, complicated, and simple ones in his Cynefin framework [90]. There, "simple" and "complicated" decisions are amenable to repeatable solutions. Chaotic situations are those which are so immediate that there is no time available for analysis as described in this book. The "complex" realm is where "wicked" problems are solved: where we do have some time to think straight, yet emergent, nonlinear, and other nonintuitive behaviors dominate, and so this is where DI is of most value.

Complexity science is a massive field, and supports helping to model both individual elements of a decision model, as well as to understand the emergent behaviors of decision models as a whole. The reference [91] is a good introductory resource.

SIMULATION, OPTIMIZATION, FORESIGHT, AND OPERATIONS RESEARCH

I love the Decision Intelligence idea of bringing a 'flight simulator' capability into the business world. I hope I'm a better business leader than I am a pilot, but if I 'crashed' my business as often as I crashed my airplane in Microsoft Flight Simulator, there would be no business left to lead.

— Jim Casart (startup advisor and serial entrepreneur [92])

So far, I've introduced the CDD as a mechanism to align multiple stakeholders around a common mental model. I also extended it, in the previous section, to show how the CDD can act as a scaffold for understanding where ML models fit into a collaboratively built model of an organization's decision.

We can imagine how we might build software based on this model, to simulate the impact of this decision, as described below.

Figure 35. Decision Model with Backward Arrow, to Illustrate Optimization.

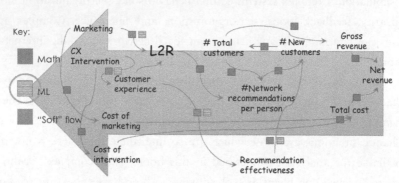

From Simulation to Optimization

From a DI point of view, simulation can be thought of as the process of experimenting with various decision levers to understand their outcomes. After they have agreed to the CDD structure, for example, the decision making team for the Ward Bank of Chapter 2 might use a computer to experiment with various decisions to see how they impact outcomes. Here, the *forward* decision model is run *backward*, as illustrated in Figure 35.

The idea here is that, once we know how levers lead to outcomes, a computer can automatically experiment with various lever settings to find the best combination. What's the best price to charge? Where should I build my new equipment? Who should receive a loan, to minimize risk? Which of my people should I train for what program? Where will my philanthropic donation have the greatest impact? These and hundreds of other decisions are informed by data, but we usually only go part of the way toward a full optimization solution, as can be achieved with this approach.[2]

Foresight

In a rapidly changing world, the ability to foresee future events is fast becoming a strategic priority for private and public institutions alike.

Says Sheila Ronis, who along with Leon Fuerth is co-directing the Rockefeller Brothers Fund's Project on Foresight and Democracy:

> *Foresight can be used to bring vision and creativity to the*
> *democratic discourse needed for the creation of sound public*
> *policy. We are gathering people who represent diverse populations*
> *within our broader society and who are deeply engaged in*
> *advocacy. Together, we will discuss the complex societal*
> *implications of oncoming major disruptors that are arising from*
> *high technology; CRISPR, artificial intelligence, the Anthropocene,*
> *genetic engineering, manipulation of mind, and more: the*
> *implications of all must be understood for effective planning. [93]*

Organizations like these and others are growing worldwide. Another example is Kedge Futures, based in Orlando, Florida, whose Launch To Tomorrow (LTT) project is described in more detail in Chapter 5. Its mission is to "[...] empower organizations and individuals to seize opportunities, achieve aspirations and turn both short- and long-term possibilities into the actions and outcomes you need today" [94].

Operations Research

Originating during World War II, the field of Operations Research (OR, also known as Operational Research and Management Science) is the discipline by which advanced analytical techniques are brought into multiple high-value use cases, "not maths in theory, but maths in the real world, making a real difference" [95, 96]. OR underlies decisions like how suitcases are to be queued to move through a new airport, how a taxi fleet positions its cars to minimize customer wait time, and more. Most of these decisions are very high value and require considerable mathematical analysis to solve.

What is the difference between OR and DI? OR is to DI as business computing is to the personal computing revolution: DI represents the democratization of advanced technology — including widely used OR techniques like simulation and optimization — into new use cases, whereas OR goes "deep" into applying decision engineering principles to problems like logistics and route planning. Another metaphor is the recent explosion of 3D printing, which is an adaptation of techniques that have been available from expensive machinery for decades.

Going forward, OR and DI have a lot to say to one another, as DI provides a mechanism for brilliant and well-proven OR techniques to be more widely used, as well as a bridge between OR and complementary technologies like deep learning and expert systems.

For instance, Ryan O'Neil works at a leading meal delivery provider whose core technology was informed by early DI writings. A former OR analyst from the MITRE Corporation, Ryan observed a gap covered elsewhere in this book, between the skills required for good quantitative modeling and those for production of software delivery. He bridged this gap by cross-training and cross-hiring: quants were required to understand production software best practices, and vice versa. Says O'Neil: "I don't expect people to have these skills when they are hired: I commit to teaching them, and this becomes a great force multiplier."

As a PhD researcher, O'Neil is today building "hybrid optimization" strategies that combine multiple technologies together to solve business problems that are worth substantial amounts of money to his employer and its restaurant partners. Going forward, he expects to combine online stochastic combinatorial optimization (OSCO) to manage the rapidly changing delivery scenario information, continually changing the system's decisions to adapt to a constant shift.

Simulation Organizations

A number of additional organizations use various kinds of decision making simulations. Here are a few brief descriptions; please follow the links in the associated bibliography entries shown to learn more.

- *World Makers*. With a focus on environmental decision making simulation, this community's goal is to "encourage people to build computer simulations of the world. This includes simulating water, weather, crops, land use policy or anything else. Models can be regional or global, simple sketches or full-blown simulations" [97]. Says community manager Anselm Hook, "My key hope is to encourage civic computer simulations of land use — like sim city, essentially games based on real data that any interested stakeholder can try ideas in. The goal is to shift civic debate away from pure rhetoric and level the playing field. Governments and corporations already have academic models that nobody can play with" [98].

- *The Silicon Valley Sim Center*. Intended to act as a center to support in-person, live DI collaboration, this Sim Center is being started by a combined team from Silicon Valley and the San Diego Sim Center [99].

- *The Center for Complex and Strategic Decisions*. Founded by Distinguished Professor of Management at Walsh College, Dr Sheila Ronis, this initiative has recently moved to Washington, DC. In its formative stages, this project was recently piloted at a government agency, and, moving forward, is targeted to help the entire federal workforce handle complexity.

- *Quantellia*. This company has built a few decision simulations, which are illustrated with both YouTube videos as well as in-browser interactive tools that you can experiment with yourself [100].

INTERDEPENDENCIES AND THE WHACK-A-MOLE

The greatest success I've had in my career building high-performance intelligent systems comes from breaking down communications barriers between different disciplines.

— Ryan O'Neil [101]

In his groundbreaking book, *Team of Teams*, Stanley McChrystal explains that, in order to succeed in a unique battlefield situation, he had to turn old habits inside-out. Military teams, he explained, had maximized their *within-team* performance, while ignoring *between-team* interfaces. "Whatever efficiencies are gained [within] silos," writes McChrystal, "are outweighed by the consequences of interface failures," meaning team-to-team connections [102].

Indeed, says McChrystal, "Task force leadership was playing 'whack-a-mole'" [103]. This is a reference to the game, popular at carnivals in the United States, where the player waits for an animal to pop up from a hole and must hit it with a hammer before it drops back into the hole. Under the table is a hidden machinery that determines the next mole to pop up. Teams were doing great at their assigned tasks but were failing due to an inability to perceive the activities of other teams in a timely and accurate manner.

A telecom CIO I interviewed told me, "Each of my divisions is making its KPIs [Key Performance Indicators, a measure of business success like a score on a customer survey], but my organization as a whole is going downhill."

This, again, is the "whack-a-mole" pattern in a nutshell: over the years complex organizations have controlled that complexity by organizing into departments, leaving the between-department relationships with less attention.

An example: the call center of a telecom company may be incentivized to spend as little time with customers as possible to resolve issues. Within the call center, this is a good idea, because it reduces costs. However, this incentive can be a bad idea for the organization as a whole: if you spend time with valuable customers, then those customers are more likely to recommend you to a friend, are less likely to leave you for a competitor, and are more likely to speak well of you on social media (a force that is becoming more and more important).

The necessity of moving from specialization to cross-specialty integration is woven thoughtfully through much of Buckminster Fuller's writings:

> *We are in an age that assumes the narrowing trends of specialization to be logical, natural, and desirable. [...] Advancing science has now discovered that* **all the known cases of biological extinction have been caused by overspecialization, whose concentration of only selected genes sacrifices general adaptability.** *[...] Specialization has bred feelings of isolation, futility, and confusion in individuals. It has also resulted in the individual's leaving responsibility for thinking and social action to others. Specialization breeds biases that ultimately aggregate as international and ideological discord, which in turn leads to war. [104] (Author's emphasis)*

Joe Brewer, who has recently moved his family to a systems-thinking-inspired sustainability hub in Costa Rica, captures the implications well:

> *We could easily let this massive clockwork of complexity overwhelm us. If it's all connected, where and how shall I intervene? Isn't it all too big for me to do anything about? Again, this is the beauty of interdependence. Tug at the right piece of frayed string and the whole rug will unravel before you. [105]*

Reiterating this point, Josh Kerbel, an analyst at the Office of the Director of National Intelligence (ODNI) speaks from his point of view in understanding complex foreign policy dynamics:

Linear reductionist approaches are significantly less useful for understanding nonlinear systems. Those systems in which the behavior of the whole is not necessarily equal to the sum of the parts [...] what is required is a complementary (not necessarily substitute) approach that is based on developing a broader, big-picture perspective- what Nobel Prize-winning physicist Murray Gell-Mann has termed a "crude look at the whole" or, in a word, a "synthesis." [11]

So, what does this mean in practical terms? If you work within a large organization whose decisions you are trying to improve, it means the low-hanging fruit of high benefit at low relative cost will probably be found in those decisions that cross *between* departments. If you are a community activist or individual, it means the best solutions are probably to be found by working with diverse teams.

In both cases, creating a shared map of how the pieces fit together to make a whole, and focusing on a decision to be made, is probably the most focused way to get started and to avoid getting lost in facts, experiences, and more that don't impact the decision at hand. This is why the CDD — or something like it — is one of the most important tools of this century.

Referring back to Figure 30, one of these things is not like the other; #5 is regarding the capacity to decide: we must understand how a decision, once made, will ripple through interdependencies — whether across the earth or across our business (or both) to impact the future. We must decide how this cause-and-effect chain warps as external circumstances shift. We must decide, and re-decide, in a complex dance.

This is one of the primary insights underlying the emergence of simulation centers internationally (as mentioned earlier), and my next key insight.

Key Insight #34: Increasingly, the problems we face are those that require us to understand interdependencies, and to re-synthesize what are otherwise stovepipes of information and initiative.

SYSTEM DYNAMICS, SYSTEMS ANALYSIS, AND SYSTEMS THINKING

The major problems of the world are the result of the difference between how nature works and how people think.

— Gregory Bateson

Why do we only have two major mobile phone operating systems: Apple and Android? Why only two major computer operating systems (Apple and Microsoft)? Why do so many of us use Google, as opposed to other search engines?. What is happening "under the covers" that leads a market, once full of many providers, to consolidate to only a few?

The answers to these and similar questions are to be found in the field of *System Dynamics*, which boasts a long history from the work of Jay Forrester at MIT [106], and Robert McNamara and the US Defense Department's "whiz kids."

Despite its power and importance however, system dynamics has received far less attention than Big Data in recent years. Plotting an interest in Google Trends shows, for example, that system dynamics (along with Complex Systems, covered later) has been eclipsed by Big Data, AI, and ML in Google searches since 2004 [107].

At its simplest, system dynamics consists of understanding chains of cause-and-effect, especially feedback loop effects. For instance, Google may have started out as a marginally better search engine than, say, Alta Vista, but its success bred more success, in a snowball effect. Similarly, military escalation in one country leads to escalation in another (Figure 36 [108]).

We might even argue that we've been "lost in data" for over a half century. Focusing on only data, however, is like trying to understand a troop of

Figure 36. Cycle of Military Escalation.

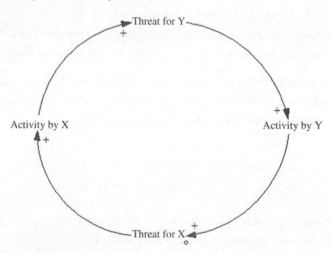

elephants by studying only their footprints: the evidence they leave behind. Understanding the elephant herself – her motivations, thoughts, and physiology – gives considerably more insights.

Before today's Big Data hype explosion, the importance of systems was more widely understood and constituted the important disciplines of system dynamics (which was promoted by Jay Forrester and continues through the System Dynamics Society [106]), systems analysis (often attributed to Robert McNamara), and systems thinking (attributed to Russell Ackoff [109] and Gregory Bateson [110]).[3]

Steve Brant, who studied with Ackoff, and who like me might be thought of as a "cyber resurrectionist" trying to reconvene these fields, wrote in 2017 that:

It is possible to solve the many crises America faces. It is possible to not just solve but dissolve our crises in education, health care, job creation, etc. But we won't do so if we keep trying to solve them the way we have [...] separately. We must solve them in the context of redesigning the larger sociological system in which they all reside.

And this is why I am urging all of you to explore the life's work of Dr. Russell Ackoff – and that of the other systems thinking theorists with whom he worked – on this, the occasion of his death. There is no more critical thing "we, the people" can do for the long-term health of our nation than to reorient how we approach solving our problems. [109]

Barry Kort says systems thinking characterizes a "ninth intelligence [...] the rarest of them all" [111]. System patterns are, of course, at the core of understanding the natural world, and circular patterns in ecosystems. Adding wolves to an ecosystem, for example, controls deer populations, which reduces grazing, which stops river erosion [112].

System Dynamics Can Trump Data

Consider *Harry Potter and the Mystery of Inequality* [113], where Alex Tabarrock writes that J. K. Rowling is the first author in history to earn a billion dollars, way ahead of Homer, Shakespeare, and Tolkien. The reason why: although the average writer's income hasn't increased in the last few years, inequality is increasing; the top is pulling away from the median. This is because of a publicity feedback effect that manifests in a highly connected society. And, says economist and game theory expert Ruth Fisher, this holds for most, if not all, entertainment industries [33].

The winner-takes-all pattern goes way beyond books [114]. And it's getting worse, everywhere. As explained by Investopedia:

> [...] the prevalence of winner-takes-all markets is expanding as technology lessens the barriers to competition within many fields of commerce. A good example of a winner-takes-all market can be seen in the rise of large multinational firms, such as Wal-Mart. In the past, a wide variety of local stores existed within different geographic regions. Today, however, better transportation, telecommunications and information technology systems have lifted the constraints to competition. Large firms like Wal-Mart are able to effectively manage vast resources in order to gain an advantage over local competitors and capture a large share in almost every market they enter. [32]

So to understand market dynamics, and to navigate effectively within them, we need more than data. We need to know which decisions – what we might call the "super levers" – will create a "butterfly effect": swinging us from winning to losing. In the face of these influences, other factors matter very little.

Market winner-takes-all effects are only one example of powerful feedback loops. *Invisible Engines* [115] exposes their hidden presence in many systems: a dynamic that, although more powerful than data, is not nearly as well hyped or widely understood.

A System Dynamics Fishing Example

French deep-sea fishermen suffer accident rates that are among the highest of all industries. To improve safety, simulations were developed studying a fleet's navigational decision making under many conditions, including weather and visibility – even the daily market price of fish. By the end of the study, the simulation results consistently matched those in the real world, and it was concluded that collisions could be all but eliminated if boats were fitted with sophisticated navigational equipment that showed the crew their exact location, and also the location of other boats nearby [116].

At first, this was an unqualified success, with collision rates falling dramatically. However, after some time, the collision rate began to rise again, eventually surpassing its original level. Another study was undertaken, this time to understand what had happened.

Nobody anticipated what this investigation would reveal, which was that, while better situational awareness had the direct effect of reducing the collision risk, it also led to higher-order effects in the causal chain that actually *increased* the number of collisions.

It turned out that, to the fishermen, knowing where other boats were located was far less a matter of safety, but one of profitability. With their new equipment, rather than having to spend costly time searching for fish, they could now head straight to the best fisheries simply by sailing to where all the "dots" (i.e., other boats) were on the anti-collision screen. Realizing this, many of the fishermen felt that making their location visible to all the other boats was giving away important competitive information to their rivals. So, they turned off their transponders, with catastrophic effect.

As it turned out, the navigation equipment created a combination of factors which, rather than preventing collisions, made them almost inevitable.

First, the "follow the dots" practice meant boats now worked in much closer proximity than they had before. Second, each crew's belief that the technology would always warn them of potential collisions lowered their vigilance. And finally, all the while, lurking among the visible "dots," there were the boats operating in "stealth mode," invisible to the technology and unknown to other crews until it was too late [117].

This misunderstanding of the causal chain of a risk reduction solution is summarized in Figure 37.

The causal model for this understanding is shown in Figure 38, below. This is a 'lobster claw' pattern that permeates systematic errors

> **Key Insight #35:** Optimizing a near-term or nearby outcome can lead to a much different unintended farther-away or longer-term outcome. Once you start looking for it, you'll find this "lobster claw" pattern of unintended consequences everywhere.

As diagrammed in Figure 39, for the fishermen, this pattern played out as follows: adding the radar system (1) was expected to have a single result: reduction

Figure 37. Without Causal Modeling, a Fisherman's Risk Reduction System Unexpectedly Increased Boat Collisions.

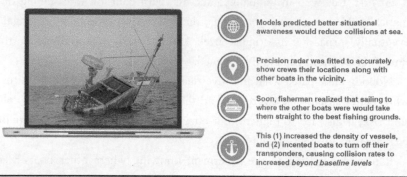

Models predicted better situational awareness would reduce collisions at sea.

Precision radar was fitted to accurately show crews their locations along with other boats in the vicinity.

Soon, fisherman realized that sailing to where the other boats were would take them straight to the best fishing grounds.

This (1) increased the density of vessels, and (2) incented boats to turn off their transponders, causing collision rates to increased *beyond baseline levels*

Figure 38. The "Lobster Claw" Causal Pattern: Near-term and Close-by Effects Are Often Radically Different than Long-term and Far-away Ones.

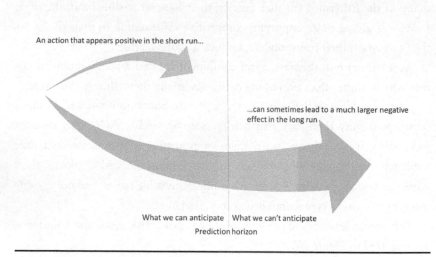

An action that appears positive in the short run...

...can sometimes lead to a much larger negative effect in the long run

What we can anticipate   What we can't anticipate
Prediction horizon

in collisions (2), which would lead to improved safety (3). But there was an unintended consequence: increased proximity from boats using others to indicate the presence of fish (4). When combined with the tendency to turn the radar off when over a school of fish (5), this led to an increase in collisions (6), which more than offset the increase in safety from the "happy path" side of the claw.

If the radar designers had taken just a few minutes to conduct a DI exercise to brainstorm through the possible impacts of introducing radar, and to

Figure 39. Qualitative Causal Model Showing the Reason for Increased Fishing Accidents from Collision Detection Devices.

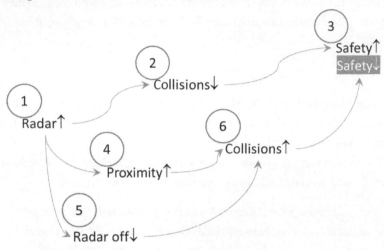

draw Figure 39, the unnecessary risk and downstream negative impacts of this decision could have been avoided.

This point is worth reiterating in the following insights.

> **Key Insight #36:** When making any decision in a complex environment, there is a huge potential benefit from taking the time to collaboratively sketch out the expected downstream impacts of a decision.

> **Key Insight #37:** There can be huge benefits from even a simple, qualitative diagram, where no data have been gathered and the diagram only depends on the expertise of persons in the industry.

I have helped dozens of my customers through this process over the years, and there is always an "aha" moment of insight as the team's multiple insights come together into a coherent diagram.

Another elephant metaphor is relevant here: called the "blind men and the elephant" parable. Four blind men approach an elephant. "What a big snake," says the first, feeling the trunk. "What a sturdy tree," says another, touching the elephant's leg. "A good rope," says the third regarding the tail. "Material for a sturdy cloak," says the fourth, touching the ears.

The elephant is much like a complex situation, where no individual understands the "big picture." So, taking the time to collaboratively draw system diagrams like Figure 39 is universally valuable. The moment your decision stakeholders realize they're touching different parts of the same "elephant" of the complex situation is powerful, intuitive, and transformative in informing their ability to work together to combine diverse information.

The Weakest Link

Strategic foresight expert Dr. Sheila Ronis says that, "No system is stronger than its weakest link. One purpose for systems analysis is to find those links, because they often can't be controlled."

The importance of systems analysis is also highlighted by W. Edwards Deming, who worked with Ronis and once wrote to her to say:

> it's important to understand how often people make the wrong decisions [...] they have all the data in the world and they don't do anything with it [...] frequently it's for political reasons that they make exactly the wrong choice, and you have to allow for that: to model it and understand it. [93]

Although there is substantial literature on the use of systems analysis in management science [118], in my experience this perspective has not made it into the minds of senior managers. Neither systems analysis as a discipline, nor the core concepts within it, are mentioned by the executives that I work with and have interviewed worldwide, even those facing the most difficult of problems that could be deeply informed by this approach. Like other academic disciplines, there is a barrier to broad adoption, to jumping the chasm from academics to widespread practice. I hope this book is part of a movement that addresses this issue. Figure 40 (which Mark Zangari explained in this video: [119]) shows a historical vision that seems to have never been realized. Our infatuation with data and analytics meant that we dropped interest in systems analysis and decisions. It's time to get back on this path.

TRANSFER LEARNING

Every year, the international ImageNet challenge pits teams from around the world to build neural network systems to rapidly and accurately recognize images. In 2015, for the first time, the performance of the winning ImageNet

Figure 40. Data Was Supposed to Be One of the Several Cooperating Disciplines. It Hasn't Made It Yet.

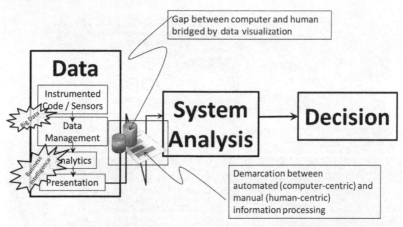

team, from Microsoft, not only beat the other competitors but also beat the best ever measured human performance on this task [120]. Part of its approach was to use a technique called *transfer learning*, which I invented in the 1980s [29, 121–123].

The basic idea of transfer learning is to use a ML model trained on one task as a starting point to learn another. So, for the ImageNet task, Microsoft researcher Jian Sun built an image recognition network in advance of the competition. It was able to learn features that are common to many images, like lines, curves, circles, and squares. And so, when presented with the images to be used for the challenge, it had an advantage over other systems, which only used the images provided for the challenge itself.

Transfer learning is essential as we build more and more sophisticated AI systems that can perform the single-link tasks that make up a multi-link decision model.

INTELLIGENCE AUGMENTATION (IA)

The future of AI is to know us, and to know our strengths and fallacies well enough to be a trusted ally.
— Charles Davis (CTO/Co-founder of Element Data [124])

Figure 41. DI Builds on Data and AI Stack but Bridges into Human-in-the-loop Use Cases.

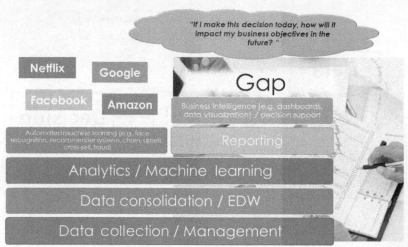

As shown in Figure 41, there are two distinct ways to use data and analytics: fully autonomously (on the left) and with a human in the loop (shown in the right). Both situations require data, analytics, and ML. Typical of fully autonomous ML systems are those that answer: "Which advertisement should I show?" "What is the best book to recommend?" "What is the best film to recommend?" But they don't answer questions that require a deeper and more complex knowledge of a world that does not yet exist: "What company should I invest in?" "What features should I offer on my new product?" "What is the best regulatory structure to achieve my social goals?"

As illustrated in Figure 42, the situations (use cases) where fully auto-mated systems are useful is a tiny subset of the full set of situations where intelligent systems can act as advisors, working hand-in-hand with humans, instead of as a substitute for them.

Yet we tend to ignore these hybrid systems; the major ML conferences (such as NeurIPS, MLconf, and more) focus on the autonomous ones at their expense.

Indeed, AI and DI pioneer Barney Pell points out that the optimal amount of automation for an AI system is somewhere between "none" and "all," as shown in Figure 43 [125].

Figure 42. The Fully Autonomous Use Cases for AI Are Only a Small Fraction of the Possibilities.

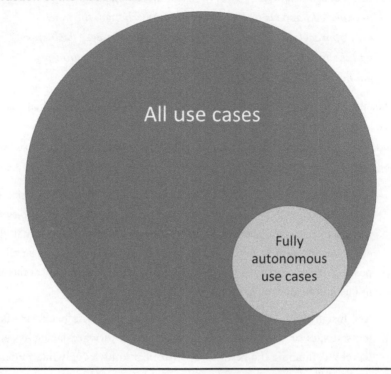

Figure 43. The Ideal Level of Automation Is neither "None" nor "All" but Somewhere In-between.

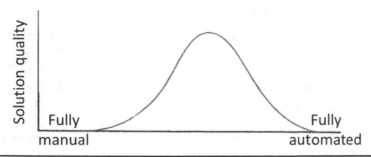

Says Opera Solutions CEO Arnab Gupta:

> *As soon as the situation becomes dynamic, when something unexpected happens and basic assumptions change, the machine-only approach fails mightily—witness the Wall Street "flash crash" and the turmoil in the mortgage market that drove the housing finance crisis in 2008. [126]*

So, the vast majority of the important problems that AI will help us to solve in the future will require humans in the loop. And to do that we must build hybrid models that combine human expertise with machine intelligence.

Key Insight #38: One way to look at DI is that it is the practice of helping humans to work with computers to address complex decisions in a way that minimizes "cognitive friction" – the goal is that the effort required for a person to work with the computer is as small as possible (this is achieved by the use of a widespread archetypal mental model and its documentation as a CDD).

Key Insight #39: DI systems allow the use of piecewise backward facing statistics or models in what is essentially a forward-facing system, thereby combining the best of our historical knowledge while mitigating the "Black Swan" [127] likelihood of being unable to respond correctly to unusual and catastrophic events.

Gupta articulates the principles of the man–machine framework as follows [126]:

- *"The machine is a prosthetic of the human mind.*
- *The computer interface supports the human thought process, not the other way around.*
- *The man-machine interface's purpose is to facilitate frontline productivity for humans in business.*
- *The best processes separate tasks into those appropriate for machines and those appropriate for humans."*

Intelligence augmentation (IA) pioneer and *Englebart Hypothesis* [128] lead author Valerie Landau says:

> *IA is within the DNA of all Silicon Valley Technologies. The reason is that, when Doug Englebart wrote the original grants to fund the ARPAnet, the ideas of augmenting human intelligence and collective IQ were central to its justification. IA is mostly unconscious, except for a few like UI pioneer Alan Kay [...] the UI ideas that came out of Xerox Parc and ultimately made their way into Apple computers and the Windows operating system all originated with Doug for whom IA was a central tenet. [129]*

DECISION ANALYSIS

With an over 30-year history, the field of decision analysis (DA) covers the philosophy, methodology, and professional practice for formally addressing important decisions. DA has been used in a wide variety of domains including pharmaceuticals, energy, and the environment, often in complex situations where multiple objectives and decisions must be made under uncertainty.

DA has a considerable overlap with DI, but with a particular focus: providing tools and techniques for teams and leaders to formalize and structure high-value decisions in complex situations. It is less technology- and data-focused than decision support, business intelligence, and DI, all of which go beyond decision making to provide tools that are used continuously in an organization.

Stanford offers a graduate certificate in DA [130], and the Society of Decision Professionals (SDP) [131] holds an annual meeting with a few hundred participants. However, the field has not grown nearly as exponentially as AI and ML have. SDP's annual meeting in 2019 is bridging this gap by focusing on the connection between DA and data science. This represents a huge potential to bridge DA, which understands best practices for human decision making teams, with the other disciplines covered here [132, 133].

POPULATING LINKS: ANALYTIC HIERARCHY PROCESS AND SKETCH GRAPHS

The analytic hierarchy process (AHP) is used by many for determining the right structure for cause-and-effect links. It's central, for example, to the work of strategic consultancy Transparent Choice [134].

To understand how AHP relates to DI, consider Figure 21, which shows a possible relationship between the number of articles a person has written and their suitability for a certain job.

This shows that a person without any publications has zero suitability, and they are a better and better fit for the job based on this criterion as their article count climbs to about 150. Above 150, publishing more articles is a liability.

But how can we obtain the shape of this graph? AHP, which was invented by Thomas L. Saaty in the 1970s [135] is an important technique to help us elicit human knowledge when it's not easy to simply draw a curve like this one.

The core of the approach is to ask a decision maker to compare two graphics at a time. For example, as described in a research study, physicians were interested in knowing what kind of graphic was best to explain cancer screening risk to patients [136]. Each patient was shown two data visualizations that illustrated the same information. Patients were asked to say, for example, "It's five times easier to understand the visualization on the left versus the right one." These data, fed to an AHP system, gave the doctors an overall preference ranking. Here, the left-hand side of the causal link was the type of visualization, and the right-hand side was the amount (e.g., "five times easier") that patients preferred it to other options. AHP tells us how to get from one to the other, as illustrated in Figure 44.

Note the similarity of this diagram to the supervised learning paradigm, where examples are used by the learning system to create a model. Here, comparison data are used by the AHP system to create a model.

This is a powerful approach in these sorts of "black box" situations where we don't have the intuition to draw a sketch graph.

Figure 44. How to Build an AHP Link.

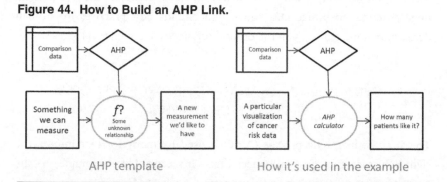

AHP template   How it's used in the example

DESIGN AND DESIGN THINKING

When creating a complex object like a building or a car, *design* is the process by which the product is envisioned before manufacturing begins. The design of a building is embodied in a blueprint; automotive design is done using a computer-assisted design (CAD) computer simulation; a movie is designed through storyboards.

It is also possible to design more abstract objects, like software. Indeed, an important breakthrough in software engineering was the use of design principles to create a number of standard diagrams that represented the complexities of a software system in advance of writing code [137]. As described in Chapter 2, DI derives much of its capabilities from other engineering disciplines.

> **Key Insight #40:** Like other engineered artifacts, decisions can be designed.

IDEO is one of the most important design and design thinking companies worldwide. It designs both tangible objects (like chairs) as well as intangible ones (like government policies).

In recent years, IDEO has acknowledged that "the future of design is circular," meaning that organizations cannot assume infinite sources of materials (such as for extractive industries like plastics) nor are there infinite sinks into which waste can be dropped (such as the ocean). Instead, the output of one system must become the input of the next, otherwise we will overextract and overpollute.

Embracing concepts like regenerative thinking, understanding circular processes, and more, IDEO, like many others, is teaching its clients about circular processes [138, 139]. For instance, a light fixture might be designed with individually replaceable components, allowing for a substantially longer life. Or a clothing company might create a "worn wear" shop to explain how to repair its products [140].

GAME THEORY

No decision is made in isolation. A choice made by Apple regarding a feature in its next iPhone impacts Google's next Android release, and the cycle continues. A government's decision to support a rebel faction in a Middle Eastern country creates ripples worldwide.

The concept of "gaming out" a decision refers to thinking through the wave of downstream moves and countermoves by competitors, allies, markets, and more. Much as in a game of chess, my best move depends on a cascade of such downstream possibilities made by my allies, adversaries, and neutral parties.

The field of game theory [141] formalizes this notion of how decisions reverberate throughout a larger system of multiple actors. As you might imagine, it is highly valuable in complex situations, yet game-theoretic analysis is not mainstream within large organizations; it is more often considered cutting-edge and its benefits are not well understood.

Game theory is an extremely valuable lens, for instance, through which to consider decisions regarding adoption or deployment of particular technology components, such as hardware or software, that function within larger technology ecosystems [142].

DI and game theory are highly complementary. A decision model that includes, as an external factor, a second decision model of choices made by a competitor is an example scenario. Game theory also benefits from DI, which supplies valuable understanding on how organizations make complex decisions.

KNOWLEDGE MANAGEMENT

DI is what KM was supposed to be. Capturing decisions, along with their rationale, is one of the most important aspects of organizational memory. It's also something most organizations are not very good at doing. DI provides a much richer framework from which to make this happen.

— Rick Ladd (formerly Pratt & Whitney Rocketdyne KM lead [143])

The job of knowledge management (KM) professionals is to ensure that organizational knowledge is available, usable, and up-to-date. Since this knowledge is often used to support decisions, KM and DI are highly complementary. Indeed, from one point of view, DI could be viewed as the subfield of KM that organizes and formalizes all knowledge that is used to make decisions.

One of the most important roles of KM is to provide a "sensor network" within an organization to alert to upcoming problems. KM expert Linda

Kemp says that, "Inattention to critical knowledge is an old problem. Lessons are forgotten, near misses are ignored, caution is dismissed, disasters result. Titanic. Bhopal. AIG. Katrina. Fukushima. And on and on" [144]. Using the 9/11 commission as an example, Kemp points out that although knowledge to avoid problems is available within many organizations, it is not always made available in such a way as to create such an alert [145].

DI may well be the missing element in KM systems today. Kemp goes on to say that:

> KM should curate, make relevant, and draw attention to timely information potentially needed for critical actions. That requires working backwards through a causal chain, providing a culture open to information sharing, and presenting the information in a way that's easily understood. Decision Intelligence is the discipline that provides this solution. As such, it offers a robust platform for KM and for a system capable of blinking red.[4]

Ladd explains the value of DI in KM in more detail as illustrated in Figure 45. This figure shows that knowledge can come from people or things, and that this knowledge can be tacit or explicit. KM's job is to support the capture of knowledge as well as to make it available when it is needed.

Figure 45. Knowledge Management Framework.

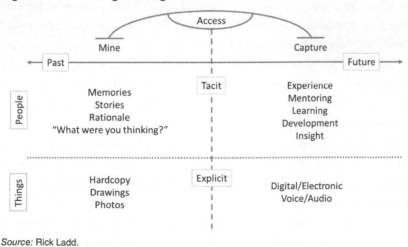

Source: Rick Ladd.

STATISTICS

Using evidence to make good decisions was traditionally the realm of the field of statistics. Today, statistics, AI, ML, and DI are deeply interwoven. Many ML techniques are based on statistical principles. Bayesian statistics are an important part of DI.

In general, statistical methods differ from AI by their focus on smaller data sets and their use of statistical assumptions as to the distribution of data. For instance, a statistical method might assume that the distribution of heights in a population follows a normal — or bell-shaped — curve. Using this assumption, a statistical method could draw reliable conclusions about an animal's height given its weight from only a few examples of "height, weight" pairs of that animal.

In contrast, ML is often used for problems for which not as much can be assumed, and so it depends on a larger amount of data as a substitute for knowledge about data distribution. Since "Big Data" is now available in many arenas, this is today practical in a way that it wasn't in the past.

Another significant difference between statistical methods and AI is that AI is usually used *retrospectively*, meaning that a data set is gathered in advance of any experimental design, and then AI is used to identify patterns in that data. Statistical methods can be used proactively as well, such as when designing a Randomized Controlled Trial (RCT) to test the efficacy of a new medicine.

Relative to DI, most statistical methods provide single-link answers, just as ML does, as was explained in Chapter 1. So, a typical statistical question might be to address a single-link question like "If I know a 10-year-old child's IQ, how will that translate into their salary at age 25?" In contrast, DI concerns itself with what's the best action to take, given this answer. For instance, given that I know the relationship between IQ and salary, what are the consequences of various choices I may make about raising that child, such as the choice of their school?

Finally, statistics does not typically concern itself with the combination of expert knowledge and data. A typical decision model is based both on human expertise (for links where data are not available), and on links where data are available.[5]

A statistical subfield that deserves special mention in this context is *Bayesian statistics* — an old field that has been experiencing a resurgence in recent years [146]. The basic idea of Bayesian statistics is this: what is the likelihood that you have cancer, given that you are a woman over 50. We don't calculate the overall probability of cancer, but rather we calculate probabilities of sub-populations like this one. Another example: what's the likelihood of your revenue growing next year given that your competitors don't launch a new marketing campaign. Again, we're asking not the overall probability but the probability conditional on some other situation holding.

Bayesian statistics is relevant to DI because there's a close relationship between propagating causation in the world and propagating probability (indeed, we might think of the observed probability as the epiphenomenon of the underlying causative link, modulo causation/correlation). So, a Bayesian model can be implemented in a decision model, in those circumstances when probability analysis is the right formalism to solve a particular problem.

RCTs, used in medicine and related fields, get closer. They ask, "If I apply this intervention, how will it change the outcome?" But to apply RCTs you need to conduct a prospective experimental study, a luxury most often not available to policymakers and organizational leaders facing complex decisions.

CONCLUSION

The technologies described in this chapter have substantial overlap, partly because it is very difficult for practitioners using one to avoid all the others. DI and the CDD are a first attempt at a synthesizing framework, which is the "business analysis" discipline of these advanced technologies: it gives us a structured method to analyze a business or organizational problem in the light of available tools, and to design how those tools will be used to make a decision.

There was a time before software engineering when coders would start a new project writing code. But as analysis and design took their rightful place within software engineering, the field matured and complex projects became possible. The same is possible for decision making in complex situations: we can organize it into an engineering discipline to control complexity and increase the effectiveness of our decisions.

NOTES

1. Here's a great video by my *Learning to Learn* coauthor, Sebastian Thrun [24], and Katie Mallone showing this "core" of supervised machine learning in action: [191].

2. You can see a video on this topic at [199].

3. This talk by Mark Zangari connects system dynamics with modern decision intelligence [192].

4. The Systems Savvy blog covers these and related topics at the intersection of systems, KM, and DI [193].

5. A good review at the next level of detail drawing the distinction between "old" and "new" (or "rebel") statistics is provided in [194]. The "new" statistics, which overlaps with machine learning substantially, has also been called "statistical learning," as explained there.

CHAPTER 4

HOW TO BUILD DECISION MODELS

[...] There is a profound disconnect between what is needed and the outcomes we are getting [...] Being rooted in reality means taking observational evidence seriously. It means finding the interpretive frameworks that adequately explain what is going on [...] And it means finding workable solutions based on the legitimate intelligence this inquiry produces. Or said succinctly, being rooted in reality means knowing what is actually going on and acting accordingly.
— Joe Brewer (Center for Applied Cultural Evolution, Costa Rica [147])

Only mind can discover how to do so much with so little as forever to be able to sustain and physically satisfy all humanity.
— Buckminster Fuller [104]

Figure 18 showed the template for a causal decision diagram (CDD), with its six parts: levers, intermediates, externals, outcomes, goals, and dependencies (represented as the lines between boxes). This chapter walks you through the process of drawing these yourself, or running a workshop to do so with collaborators, after some preliminary material below.

THIS MATERIAL IS USEFUL AT MULTIPLE LEVELS

There are nine levels at which you can engage with decision intelligence (DI), as follows:

(1) *Understanding*: Even if you never build a CDD, it can be valuable to use DI principles. Simply understanding that a decision is a thought process

regarding levers that lead through a cause-and-effect chain to outcomes can make you a better decision maker and help you to overcome many classic decision making mistakes, as listed near the end of this chapter.

(2) *Mapping*: Draw the CDD, once. If you take the time to do this, your chances of a good decision and avoiding unintended consequences will increase.

(3) *Sharing*: Share a CDD with others, to align your mental models and to understand a diversity of opinions, which leads to better decisions. What were, before, different mental models of the key elements of a situation turn into a shared one. This alignment has tremendous power.

(4) *Continuous improvement*: Keep the CDD up-to-date and, over time, reality and our understanding of it drifts. A CDD can be used to continuously realign you or your team, even if it is never implemented in an automated system.

(5) *Implementation*: Go beyond a CDD to create an automated decision "sandbox" simulation environment that helps you to understand the implications of your decisions. As I described in Chapter 3, one of the great promises of DI is that it allows us to work together with technology to find the "sweet spot" decision that satisfies the goals of many stakeholders, including the potential to solve "tragedy of the commons" problems.

John Seely Brown says that World of Warcraft teams make the best employees [148]. Why: working together in a complex interactive software system that represents how decisions play out over time is very powerful.

(6) *Integration*: Use the CDD to integrate multiple technologies into the decision. Typically data aren't available for the whole model, so decision modeling shows us how cutting-edge technology can augment our intuition, knowledge, and experience.

(7) *Scenario comparison*: Set up different sets of external factors to see how the same decision produces different results under different assumptions.

(8) *Optimization*: Run the decision model "backward" to use the computer to help to find the best decision in different circumstances.

(9) *Real-time decision model tracking*: Maintain a *decision impacts dashboard* as part of a decision support/business intelligence program. This system can, for example, track when assumptions enter a "yellow" or "red zone": where externals/context/scenario data are drifting so far out of their expected ranges that the decisions originally chosen will actually lead to different outcomes, triggering the need for a new simulation run.

WHO BENEFITS FROM DECISION MODELS?

The greatest hope and insight comes from those who weave threads of diversity of thought into a common cloth.
> — Dave "Tex" Smith (Chief Digital Officer,
> Da Vinci Co-op)

A number of situations might motivate you to learn how to model decisions:

- You are a senior executive responsible for ensuring that *AI/ML* is used to maximum value throughout your organization (see more on this topic below).

- You are a non-expert, wishing to effect some important *social change* (such as impacting people's decisions about the climate).

- You are a senior executive, facing a new or ongoing — perhaps struggling — *project* with a lot of data and/or human expertise (note that data are NOT necessary), yet you haven't fully understood the structure of the decision you are supporting (you'll see an example of this in the DEEPM section below).

- You are an *individual*, facing a decision in a complex situation in your life (Should I change jobs? Should I go back to school?)

- You are a *politician*, wishing to use information and expertise from your constituents and assistants to create policy.

- You are inundated with *data* and want to know how it might be used to drive value for yourself or your organization. You may have "spreadsheet-itis," characterized by giant spreadsheets that are no longer the right fit for your situation.

- You are a *business manager* holding an analytics/machine learning (ML) team accountable for providing business value, and you struggle to understand their detailed technical jargon.

- You are a senior executive looking to instill DI throughout your organization because you recognize that it, like business process management (BPM) or project management, is a powerful *competency* with broad value.

- You are a *consultant*, looking to assist a team or individual with a complex decision.

The method here applies to all of the above situations. It is important to re-emphasize: decision modeling does *not* require data. Indeed, starting this process with a large data set can lead to a "searching for the keys under the lamppost" problem. The decision model, when complete, will guide you to which data, and which fields, are the most valuable. It can (and has), in this way, save millions of dollars and years of effort cleansing or processing unnecessary data (I call this avoiding "gratuitous data management").

A side note: in the above sense, decision modeling is a natural successor to Expert Systems of the past, with a focus on situations that require decisions that lead to actions in complex environments, and providing a link between expert knowledge and data.

Decision modeling is best-suited for situations where you have multiple choices as well as multiple outcomes in a complex environment. For instance: "I want to choose to sell product A, B, or C so as to grow net revenues by 2% per year while also reducing our company's carbon footprint."

DECISION MODELING BENEFITS

Decision modeling helps you:

- To *align* a team around a common mental model of the decision.

- To discover points of greatest *leverage* in a decision. What decision, once made, will have the maximum benefit with the least cause?

- To discover *shared goals* and synergistic solutions in situations that would otherwise appear as conflicted. Decision modeling has the ability to identify the "holy grail" decisions that maximize the interests of multiple stakeholders.

- To avoid *unintended consequences*.

- To act as a "blueprint" for the insertion of *advanced technologies* like AI, ML, optimization, and more into organizations.

- To form a basis for *continuous improvement*, because the CDD is updated over time as more and more is known about the situation.

- To determine where will be the *greatest value in gathering data*. All data are not alike: some have a much greater impact on a decision outcome than others, and so gathering data in advance of building a decision model can lead to substantial wasted time. For instance, we may realize through decision modeling that it doesn't matter if our competitor charges $1 or $10 for a product: I'll still make the same decision, so refining this number further is not of value.

- To determine where will be the greatest value in obtaining additional *expertise*/facts. A similar argument to the above one applies here: for instance, we may realize through decision modeling that determining the color of our competitor's product is surprisingly very important.

SOME DECISION MODELING EXAMPLES

Imagine a domino that, once toppled, starts a chain reaction. You have a number of starting dominos to choose from, each of which leads to a different path. So the cause-and-effect chain moves forward in time from the levers to the outcomes. You want to choose the starting domino that leads to the best one. So while the result of decision modeling is a choice of levers, the process of doing that modeling is to simulate a process in time that begins with the decision and the action representing the lever.

By convention, we draw levers on the left and outcomes and goals on the right, as I showed in Figure 18.

A few examples will help to further ground this idea. Imagine a retail store chain is seeking to decide whether to install solar panels on its roofs. This decision will have an impact not only on costs to the business for the panels but also on savings in payments to the electrical grid down the road.

Or an African country is looking to cure AIDS. How much should it spend on medicine, and how much on training health care professionals to teach their patients how to use the medicine? This is a tough decision, because every dollar spent on training reduces the supply of life-saving medicine. Yet, the medicine's effectiveness will be drastically reduced if doctors aren't taught how to teach their patients how to take it at just the right time every day [150].

What about a product manager at a new software company? She has to choose the right price for the product and the right launch market. To make this choice, she'll model (either between her ears or with DI) how the price will drive purchasing behavior, how the choice of market will drive launch costs and will interact with the price, and more.

One of the most widespread kinds of levers are investment decisions: how much to spend to launch which new initiative? Investments usually result in going "into the red" in the short term, in order to reap long-term benefits. So a good model – whether in the brains of investors or modeled explicitly using software – is essential to success.

As you can see, each of these *decision levers* is effectively a choice to be made. And the choice of the right lever is the goal of decision modeling. What's different about this approach compared to many others is that the choice is the prime mover in a complex system of cause and effect, which may include feedback effects, chaotic behavior, and strange attractors.

Before talking about decision models, though, I have to chip away a little more at the data mythology.

DECISION INTELLIGENCE AND DATA

I rode the train on a beautiful spring day through New England. Arriving at the station, the gentlemen from our partner company greeted me happily; we were going to win this one. We chatted about the customer on the drive across town: "They're really turning over a new leaf"… "Very innovative"… "Hungry for new ideas."

When we arrived, it was a big meeting: as usual there were staff members from several departments, some who hadn't met each other before. The IT guys carried stacks of paper: the data model… the spreadsheets. As usual, the first part of the meeting was a chance for everyone to have their say.

And, as sometimes happens, it was mostly about data. Our customer took us through a great database schema on the whiteboard... his colleague handed out reports. Great!

"The decision is only as good as the data that supports it," said their data analyst. Someone usually does. But it's not always true.

Here's what happens: as we get into decision modeling engagements like these, we realize that all data aren't created equal: some fields matter a lot... some not so much. And often human expertise, where there's no data, makes all the difference.

The most extreme example of this comes from winner-takes-all effects that dominate national economies, markets, and more, as I described in Chapter 3. So a lot of the data that you might spend millions to gather, cleanse, and display are irrelevant to your competitive advantage, especially for "big decisions" [151]. (That being said, though, it is important to effectively manage data that *does* matter.)

Says Judea Pearl, in *The Book of Why*:

> We live in an era that presumes that big data is an answer to all of our problems [...] yet data are profoundly dumb. Data can tell you that the people who took a medicine recovered faster than those who did not take it. But they can't tell you why. Maybe those who took the medicine did so because they could afford it, and would have recovered just as fast without it. Over and over again in science and in business, we see situations where mere data are not enough. [152]

And that New England customer: I'm happy to say we won the work and went on to be invited back half a dozen times for follow-on projects. Their giant database: not needed. Our modeling work distilled their highest-value use case down to a single spreadsheet, with one table about a megabyte in size, and a few dozen fields. We focused our data governance on those fields. That's all that was needed to drive an analysis that earned the customer a bundle.

DIVERGENT VERSUS CONVERGENT THINKING

As background to several of the model-building steps I'll describe below, it's important to understand that you will engage in two different kinds of thinking: the brain uses fundamentally different processes for brainstorming – or "divergent" thinking – compared to analysis. I know that for myself, and for the teams I work with, it feels like individual or group IQ and creativity lower to about half their normal levels if you try to do both at once. FMRI studies show that these two kinds of thought use different parts of the brain and that blood sloshes from one to the other when switching [153].

For this reason, one of the most important elements of effective decision modeling is to clearly separate the divergent from the convergent parts of the process. The goal of the divergent phase, whether it's applied to outcomes, levers, externals, intermediates, goals, or dependencies, is to generate as many ideas as possible, including the bad ones. Because people will be suggesting bad ideas, it is essential to create a safe, collaborative environment. How to do so is beyond the scope of this book, but there are excellent resources on this topic.

A side note: divergent-versus-convergent thinking is related to the System 1 versus System 2 thinking described by behavioral economists, most notably Daniel Kahneman in *Thinking Fast and Slow* [26]. System 1 thought processes are intuitive; System 2 is analytical. The "breathe out, breathe in"/convergent/divergent alternation used in decision modeling unites these two elements to provide the best of both worlds.

> **Key Insight #41:** Decision modeling combines the best of divergent and convergent thinking to maximize the quality of the decision model.

BUILDING A DECISION MODEL

This section describes how to build a decision model. The steps are shown in Figure 46.

Setup

The best decision modeling team is a diverse one. Often I work with teams from multiple departments whose work is interdependent; yet, those relationships were never effectively mapped, leading to a "whack-a-mole" problem as described in Chapter 3.

Figure 46. Decision Modeling Steps.

1. Setup
2. Starting the meeting
3. Brainstorming outcomes (divergent)
4. Brainstorming levers (divergent)
5. Analyzing outcomes and goals (convergent)
6. Analyzing levers (convergent)
7. Brainstorming externals and information sources (divergent)
8. Wiring up the model: for each lever/outcome combination, develop the full chain (convergent)
9. Using the model

A side note: for the sake of brevity, the language below refers to a team of decision modelers working collaboratively for a commercial project, because this is the scenario most familiar to me. You can also use this method working alone, as described above, although you'll get the best value out of the approach if you ask a diverse team of trusted friends to review your model. It also applies for small independent teams, universities, nonprofits, governments, and more.

Also, note that a CDD can also be used for multiple decisions. It often represents key causal flows in an organization through which multiple decisions flow and so can be repurposed as appropriate in new situations.

I set up five key ingredients at the start of a decision modeling session:

(1) Plenty of whiteboard space and markers.

(2) Plan for lots of breaks, at least every hour. Remember that an important part of our goal is to learn as much from the team as possible, and so helping them to think clearly is essential.

(3) If possible, I ask a person from my team to act as "scribe." Their job may be to capture "parking lot" issues that belong later in the meeting, key open questions, or to start building a decision model in an interactive tool. The scribe may also be assigned the role of timekeeper, enforcing breaks.

(4) An executive sponsor: even five minutes from the person funding or supporting the effort at its start is very helpful. They should state the objective of the process. I often ask them to explain, "If this is a perfect

meeting, in my opinion, here's what I'd like to see as the result, and here's how it will benefit the organization as a whole."

(5) A happy, relaxed, and playful atmosphere is most conducive to effective decision modeling [154, 155]. Strive in yourself to remain nonjudgmental and positive, modeling this attitude to the meeting attendees. To the extent that it is possible to help people to feel at ease, exercises that encourage this shift are a good investment of time. Simply going around the table and asking everyone to introduce themselves and their goals for the workshop is a reasonably quick step that is often overlooked. Or you may feel that a team-building exercise is merited.

Decision modeling rarely takes less than a half day and can stretch into a week for a complex decision. I don't recommend going longer than a week at a time; the team needs time to absorb and process what has been learned. For a complex decision, you might do a follow-up session to review the decision model and/or to create sub-models.

Starting the Meeting

To start decision modeling, begin with a simple statement of the decision you are facing. Examples are "We want to learn how to use data to reduce conflict in Liberia," "I want to decide what college to attend," or "My team is launching a new product and we can't decide what price to charge and what features to offer." As an example here, I'll use a fictional company that is based on several projects. It's called AC telecom (ACT), and the decision statement is:

> We're launching a new data plan for our mobile phones. Should we offer an all-you-can-eat pricing option?

Determining the Project Rules of Engagement

The executive sponsor mentioned above may wish to state the rules of engagement, and it is important to understand the difference between executive *suggestions* and *constraints*. For instance, the executive sponsor may say that "$50 per month might be a good price for an unlimited plan." Given his position in the company, the team may believe that this is a firm constraint rather than a simple suggestion. Be sure you know which is the case.

Figure 47. Decision Making Example Rules of Engagement.

Unlimited Usage Plan

Goals and constraints for today

Determine the following aspects of a monthly unlimited mobile telephone service:

- Price of the new service

- Inducements offered (e.g. free handset)

- Contract Period, and

- Target demographic (limited to US markets) and marketing plan

- Amortization period for startup costs

Or the executive sponsor may say "I think it would be best to launch first in the United States, and then to launch in Europe later." This constraint may indeed be a "hard" one: she has the knowledge to which the team does not have access indicating that we must launch first in the United States. Ask a question like: "If our team was able to discover that we could achieve greater revenue at lower risk by launching first outside the US, would you be open to that?" If the answer is "no," then this is a hard constraint, and should be documented, perhaps on the whiteboard as shown in Figure 47.

Brainstorming Outcomes

If you don't know where you're going, any road'll take you there.
— George Harrison [156]

After a few minutes explaining the goal for the meeting, the first question I asked the team was "what are you trying to achieve with this pricing option?" This is a divergent phase, so I explained the rules of brainstorming and encouraged the team to say their ideas out loud. You might also ask people to write down their ideas on post-it notes: this can help to ensure that less assertive people are heard.

The first set of answers were as follows. I wrote these on the right-hand side of the whiteboard in a column:

- improve customer experience; and

- have a successful product launch.

A quick aside at this point: note that, for this team, I didn't teach them about DI as you've read in this book so far. Instead, we jumped straight into decision modeling. You'll want to use your judgment here: sometimes, it can help to establish your credibility and authority to spend some time teaching about Big Data, ML, and DI. This can be especially attractive if the team includes members who are passionate about AI and/or ML and are looking to expand their knowledge. I would be less inclined to conduct such a training session in advance for a team that is comprised strictly of non-technical business professionals.

> **Key Insight #42:** To build a decision model with a team, you don't necessarily need to teach them anything first: this method is such a natural fit to the usual way that people think about decisions that it is comfortable for anyone.

Tangibles and Intangible Goals and Outcomes

> *Not everything that counts can be counted, and not everything that can be counted, counts.*
>
> — Erik Brynjolfsson [157]

I continued the brainstorming session, asking "does anybody have more ideas?" I suggested in particular that they think about *intangibles* — factors that may be harder to measure but often drive the success of a company. Typical intangibles are morale, trust, and happiness [158]. They answered:

- maintain employee morale;

- fit within our environmental impact policy constraints;

- create positive social benefit; and

- help to reduce income inequality worldwide.

Figure 48. List of Goals.

```
                    Unlimited Usage Plan

                                    Goals
                    1. Improve customer experience
                    2. Have a successful product launch
                    3. Maintain employee morale
                    4. Fit within our environmental impact
                       policy constraints
                    5. Create positive social benefit
                    6. Help to reduce income inequity
                       worldwide
```

Note that this team chose to express goals here and not outcomes. Since the distinction between them[1] is not relevant here, I don't make much of a big deal out of it.

It is important to let brainstorming run its course and only to stop after a substantial silence from the team.

> **Key Insight #43:** Don't forget to elicit intangibles: they are often the "hidden gems" that drive the results of a decision in directions that are hard to anticipate unless they are explicitly discussed.

At this point, the whiteboard looked like Figure 48. The left-hand side is intentionally left blank to give space for levers.

Brainstorming Levers

Decision *levers* represent the choices than can be made to achieve the outcomes. As with outcomes, brainstorming levers is a powerful technique that can surface great ideas that would otherwise be hidden from a team of experts.

For the mobile strategy team, several of the levers had been specified by the executive sponsor, so we started by writing those on the board:

- pricing;

- services included;

- contract period; and

- inducements.

Figure 49. Levers and Goals.

Unlimited Usage Plan	
Levers	**Goals**
1. Pricing	1. Improve customer experience
2. Services included	2. Have a successful product launch
3. Contract period	3. Maintain employee morale
4. Inducements	4. Fit within our environmental impact
5. Marketing/advertising	policy constraints
6. Competitive marketing / advertising	5. Create positive social benefit
7. Encouraging likelihood-to-recommend (L2R)	6. Help to reduce income inequity
8. Competitor offers same product, but at a	worldwide
higher rate.	
9. Better customer experience	

I then asked, "what else"? The team brainstormed and wrote a few additional items on the whiteboard:

- marketing/advertising;

- competitive marketing/advertising ("we have this, the others don't");

- encouraging likelihood-to-recommend (L2R; people recommending the service to their friends);

- competitor offers the same product, but at a higher rate; and

- better customer experience.

At this point, the whiteboard looked like Figure 49.

Analyzing Levers

After a period of silence, we decided that there were no more ideas from brainstorming, so we analyzed the above elements. We first agreed that marketing/advertising and competitive marketing were probably the same thing, so collapsed that into a single category.

I then challenged whether "Competitor offers same product" was really a lever that we had control over. We agreed that this was an *external*, not a lever, so moved it to a new list for later.

Key Insight #44: Externals and levers are easy to confuse. Be sure that all levers listed can be controlled, and that all externals listed, cannot (though in a software tool you might experiment with changing them to reflect different assumptions).

I then respectfully challenged that "better customer experience" was a lever, because we can't directly impact it. On a new whiteboard, we did a "how chain" exercise: we add elements to the left on the diagram: upstream on the causal chain. I asked *how* are you going to achieve better customer experience?" They said that they could invest in training call center personnel and also increase the number of call center personnel. I asked the "How" question, again, and we agreed that these elements were as far to the left as could be possible. So, we added two items to the list:

- invest in call center training; and

- invest in more call center personnel.

I then added a link from these two items to an intermediate value, called "customer experience." So the board now looked like Figure 50.

Key Insight #45: The "how chain" consists of checking that levers are really things that can be changed. If not, ask "how" to go upstream through the causal model.

Figure 50. The Customer Experience "How Chain."

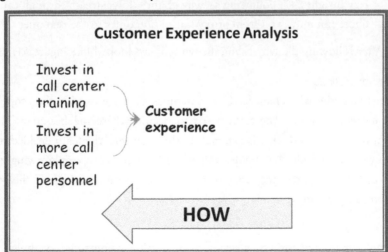

Note that, as your situation changes through time, your degree of responsibility may shift. For this reason:

> **Key Insight #46:** As system boundaries change, levers can become externals and vice versa.

Convergent Phase: Analyzing Outcomes and Goals

I then turned to the outcomes and goals. I asked the team to discuss customer experience as a goal:

> *I know how you can improve customer experience, just write a check for $1,000 to all customers. So I don't think that customer experience improvement is your end goal. It's probably more complicated than that. Understanding how this all fits together is why we're here.*

The team agreed, yes of course.

So then I asked "*why* is customer experience important?" The answer was "to ensure a successful product launch." Then I asked, "how would you know that you had a successful product launch?"[2] The answer: if it generated positive revenues. I asked again, "*Why* is it important to improve revenues?" "So we can improve our profits." And, again, why? "So we can provide shareholder value and keep the company growing and successful."

> **Key Insight #47:** Following a "why chain" downstream through causal effect can move you from proxy (false) outcomes to the real ones.

After following the why chain, the whiteboard looked like Figure 51.

Decision Boundary

Sometimes, the why chain leads to outcomes that are outside the scope of the current decision. The team needs to decide where the boundary is — what is in scope and what is external. In this example, the team decided that "So we can provide shareholder value and keep the company growing and successful, is outside" the scope of the current decision and pared the why chain back to "So we can improve our profits."

Proxy Goals

Some terminology and an extension of this rather commercial example into a much larger context: In this example, "customer experience" is what's

Figure 51. Adding the Customer Experience "Why Chain."

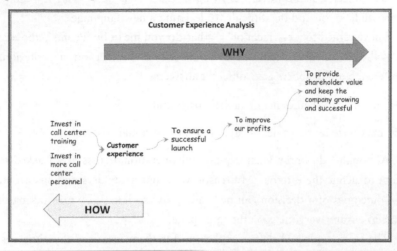

called a "proxy goal." Proxy goals were introduced in Chapter 1 and illustrated in Figure 6. It's something that may be easier to measure or manage, but there is a gap between a proxy and a true goal.

Proxy goals are dangerous and misleading if they're not identified. For instance, most of the world treats money as a proxy for happiness. Yet recent research shows that this is not true, and that there is a complicated relationship between the two. Simply learning the incorrectness of the money/happiness proxy could go a tremendous way in improving the human race [159].

And here's a homework assignment: listen today for a friend who might explain a "why" or say "because." Usually the answer to "why" is because it starts a chain of events, moving left-to-right on a CDD like the one shown above.

Also note that I asked the team to clarify "have a successful product launch." You should test each element in a decision diagram against the question: "Is this measurable enough that I would be willing to place a bet on it, and know who won the bet?" This statement isn't measurable in this way, so I asked for the clarification. The answer, "positive revenues," isn't all the way there, but it's on the way.

A final note on this process: note that my goal was to extract the team's understanding of their decision in a *language that was familiar to them.*

Many older methods require the team to learn, and then shift to, an unfamiliar language. Collaboratively drawing a CDD is a hard task; it becomes impossible if you add the difficulty of learning a new language.

I next turned to a clarification, "What do you mean by 'Profits', above? It is still too ambiguous, and doesn't meet the 'I'd bet on it' criterion." Different team members gave different answers:

(1) maximize revenues net of capital costs; and

(2) maximize revenues net of capital plus operational costs.

Although I do know what capital and operational costs are, I asked the team to define these terms. My reason was that misunderstandings around the outcomes of a decision can be deadly, and so it's well worth taking the time to ensure everyone is on the same page.

The team explained that capital costs for them were the one-time costs required to get the new pricing plan out the door. And that operational costs were the ongoing monthly costs required to keep it going, paying for things like customer care, the technical systems to allow people to use unlimited data on their phones, and advertising.

A conversation then ensued among the team as to whether (1) or (2) was the proper goal for the project. I asked them, in addition to this discussion, to decide (1) at what point would they measure the profit (two years? three years?), and (2) could they define "maximize"?

At this point, as often happens, it was important for me to keep quiet, while the team worked through this discussion. After a couple of hours, and a few breaks for side conversions, the team decided that their goals were to:

• achieve 2% net profit on this new product net of capital investment after 18 months;

• ensure that employee morale among the implementation team stayed above a score of 80%, as measured on a standardized questionnaire; and

• ensure that the environmental impact of the initiative, as assessed by a standard corporate tool, remains within allowable limits.

Note that sometimes it's helpful to distinguish the *outcome* – the value to be measured – from the *goal*, which is the value of the outcome that is acceptable. The outcome in this statement is "net profit on this new product net of capital investment after 18 months." The goal is "2%." This kind of

Figure 52. Customer Experience How and Why Chains.

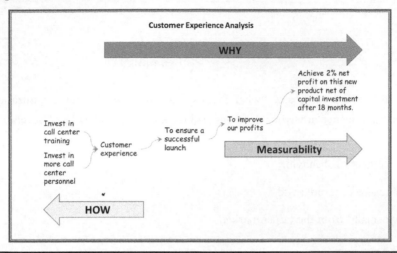

distinction is sometimes worth bringing up, sometimes not. For instance, the team may agree to the outcome and then debate the goal: what if some team members think we need to aim for 4% instead of 2%?

At this point, the customer experience *how* and *why* chains looked like Figure 52.

Collecting Out-of-context Comments Respectfully
During the discussion above, there were a number of out-of-context comments:

- The database expert told us that she had a table of information about employee morale.

- A marketing person said that he could improve social goals by marketing to low-income households at initial product launch.

- A call center expert said that he could use his team of retrained coal miners to help launch the product, thereby supporting the effectiveness of diverse resources within the company.

Although these were all great ideas, none of them are about outcomes; instead, these are levers and externals. It is natural that these comments will arise during a meeting. Although they are not on track for the outcomes brainstorming, it's important to respectfully capture them for later, to re-explain that they are not outcomes, and then to return to the task at hand.

Brainstorming Externals

I then asked the team, "what factors from outside of your organization might influence how your decisions lead to outcomes." They listed several:

- competitor behavior;

- macro economy; and

- demand from the target market.

The team began to discuss whether a major competitor would or would not also launch an unlimited pricing plan. This kind of discussion can become heated, and counterproductive, since it is based on the expertise and experiences of the team members, which are by definition different one from the other. I explained that, as we move forward with modeling, there are two ways to resolve these kinds of differences:

- It may be that the outcomes don't depend on competitors. This conversation is best to have after we're sure that it's worth having.

- We can record different opinions about competitor behavior in the model, and we can later run the model under different assumptions/ scenarios.

In decision modeling, an *assumption* is an external factor about which we have some uncertainty. A *scenario* is a set of choices about multiple assumptions in which we may run the model to see the result.

We then talked about the macroeconomy. One team member said that if consumer-spending was low, this would reduce the likelihood to purchase this plan. Another said that he'd read a paper predicting that consumer spending will continue to decrease for the next 18 months.

I explained that an external can represent an assumption about a specific point in time or can be represented as a prediction over time.

Wiring up the Model

We took a lunch break at this point, during which my scribe and I cleaned up the model to prepare for the afternoon meeting (Figure 53). As the team returned, it looked like Figure 53.

I then asked, "what chain of events from actions to outcomes do you think will have the biggest impact on your goals?" One team member answered: "Well, our operating margin depends on our costs and our revenues. So we drew some *intermediates* to capture this, as follows (Figure 54).

Figure 53. The Cleaned up Model.

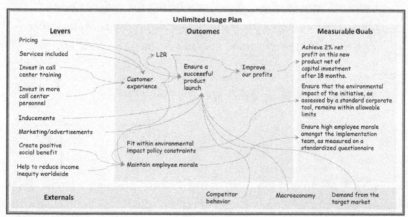

Figure 54. Enhancing the Decision Model: Adding Intermediate Values.

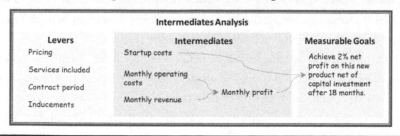

CDD workshop facilitator Håkan Edvinsson comments on his role in helping a team to create the links within the CDD. He says:

> *A challenge I have experienced is that people have no problems with the first rightmost intermediates. But when connecting them to the outcomes people tend to turn into "design mode" as they are not very secure at this step.*
>
> *I think this is when the facilitator needs to be creative and needs to be some steps ahead of the group.*
>
> *My guess is that when the operational perspectives (left part of the model) meets the managerial (right part of the model), we encounter a gap between people's viewpoints and perspectives. Executive managers may have knowledge gaps in the cause and effects patterns even in their own organisation, and also the other way around — the operatives may not be aware with the effects their daily work is causing.*
>
> *And that's what facilitation really is about. [43]*

Breadth before Depth

A question arises around this point in any decision modeling exercise: should we dive down into the details ("depth first") or should we build chains from decisions to outcomes ("breadth first")? For example, we might choose to diagram a sub-model that splits out the different components of startup costs.

In general, I've learned that it's better to go breadth-first. The reason is that the cross-model picture is usually less well-understood. The elements of startup cost (updates to sales, updates to customer care, and the like) are typically well-understood within a particular department. The great value of the initial decision modeling exercise as we are doing here is to help different departments understand their interdependencies.

This is worth reiterating: it can be tempting to "boil the ocean" by modeling every detail. Keep in mind the adage that "every model is wrong, some models are useful" and remember that your goal is to build a model that is good enough to drive alignment and an improvement to decision making and *not* to capture every detail.

Figure 55. Refining the Levers.

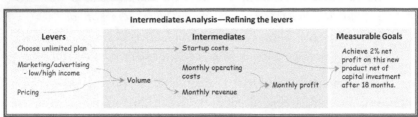

In the project described here, I chose to work breadth-first, so I next asked "what, in your best judgment, is the most influential chain of events from actions to outcomes?" In reply, one team member explained to me that offering an unlimited plan would create a substantial reduction in operational costs, because it would no longer be necessary to track minutes of use within the billing system, nor to maintain technology that handles the scenarios where a user runs out of their allotted minutes (rollover to the next month, service cutoff, and more).

We realized that this was going to be a benefit no matter what choices we made about the unlimited plan we made, so added a new lever, called "choose unlimited plan" to the left-hand side of the diagram, and linked from it to startup costs.

Then, a marketing team member said that they thought that some targeted advertising might be particularly effective in selling this plan. He said that he thought that a high-priced version of this plan might be targeted to high-income subscribers, who might be willing to pay more for a service that they didn't have to worry about. So we added a subcategory to marketing spend and linked it to volume and pricing (Figure 55).

Determining the Role of Machine Learning

An ML expert in the room then spoke up for the first time. She said:

> *I think we can do one better than that. I know that machine learning has shown a lot of promise in personalized medicine, where different treatments are recommended for different people based on gender, age, test results, DNA, and more. I think the same sort of situation applies here. And I have a data set from a similar*

product where we price tested several different pricing levels on several thousand prospects with different characteristics. I bet I could use that data set to give you an initial model of how different pricing decisions would lead to different product demands, kind of a machine-learning-based precision demand estimator.

This suggestion received a mixed response: some said it sounded edgy and expensive, but others pointed out that getting this product offering right would ultimately be worth billions to the company, so such an effort may well be worthwhile. We tabled a final decision on this question for later, and I suggested a simpler solution for now: I drew Figure 56.

I then asked anyone in the room who felt they had some insight into this relationship to draw a curve relating these two numbers. After some back and forth, we settled on the curve shown in Figure 57.

This completes my description of our decision modeling session. Additional steps you might take include the below:

- *Find feedback loops*: As described earlier, these often have the greatest impact.

- *Identify more intangibles*: These are often overlooked yet have an important impact.

Figure 56. How Does the Number of Subscribers Depend on the Price We Charge?

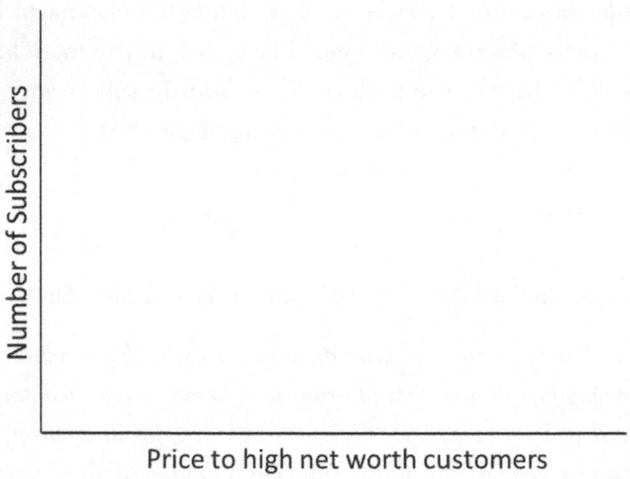

Number of Subscribers

Price to high net worth customers

Figure 57. Price Graph as Drawn.

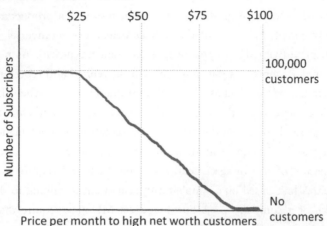

- *Conduct sensitivity analysis*: Which missing pieces of information will have the greatest impact on how actions lead to outcomes?

- *Identify constraints*: Are there values on intermediates that are simply not possible, given what we know about the world?

- *Prioritize outcomes*: Which outcomes are the most important? How will multiple outcomes be combined into a final way to measure the value of your decision?

- *Prioritize levers*: Which levers have the most impact on your outcomes? What research can you do to better understand the impact that each lever will have on the important outcomes?

- *Assign responsibility*: To improve the decision model over time, you may wish to assign a responsible person to each of its elements to research and refine it.

- *Distribute the diagram*: Sending the diagram around your organization, displaying it on a monitor in the lobby, and showing it on a business decision dashboard that can be displayed by all are all valuable tools for aligning complex decisions across your business.

- *Reconvene and refine over time/multiple versions*: A CDD is a "living" document. Refine it, use it, and repeatedly improve it over time.

To expand on the final topic: core to effective collaborative decision design is an *iterative refinement* process, where the design begins as a rough sketch to which detail is gradually added. For instance, a product's demand curve may initially be represented simply as demand being inversely proportional to price (with the proportionality constant unknown). As more data are acquired, or more analysis done, this can be refined and represented as a curve that can be sketched as a hand-drawn graph; finally, when the model is complete, these approximations may be replaced by a mathematical function that precisely describes the model's representation of the demand curve.

There may be disagreement about the shape of the links. And, depending on the nature of this disagreement, resolving them will require a different approach. A link based on a simple formula may mean talking to the financial office of a company ... A link based on ML may require that a new model be built ... a link based on knowledge of a sketch graph may require human expertise. Facilitating these disagreements is a huge and important subject and goes beyond the scope of this book. Two high-level insights are worth capturing:

> **Key Insight #48:** One of the most important contributions of the CDD is to allow disagreements about its parts to happen one at a time, in a structured way that keeps the focus on collaboratively creating the best diagram possible, instead of on competitively disagreeing with each other.

> **Key Insight #49:** Sometimes, a disagreement may be irrelevant, because precise selection of a decision has little impact on the outcome. Being able to see the flow of a decision can allow team members to avoid unnecessary time and effort in reaching an agreement about details, while still allowing them to find consensus about the decision to make.

For an example of the second insight above, the CDD may help the team to realize that it doesn't matter whether a competitor's price will be $10 or $15, because we will make the same decision either way. Avoiding unnecessary precision in this way can be a huge time-saver!

Using the Model

Once the decision diagram has been built and the workshops have been held, what's next? Who makes the decision? A decision model is always imperfect and incomplete, so there will always be hidden factors that influence the decision. So it is unreasonable to expect full consensus on the decisions to be made, simply because all team members will not be on the same page. The model can be built collaboratively, and by doing so the person responsible for the final decision will be better informed and will probably do a better job of making good decisions, using data and AI as inputs in an unbiased way, and avoiding unintended consequences.

> **Key Insight #50:** A decision model can serve as an advisory tool to a person responsible for a decision.

Some criticize decision models because they cannot possibly capture all the details of a situation. This is not their purpose. A CDD is always incomplete: by necessity and through practicality, it must leave out information that you and your team have gained through years of experience and which you know subconsciously, "in your gut," but which is difficult or impossible to articulate.

The goal is simply to do better than has been done in the past: by using a shared decision model, including shared outcomes and a shared understanding of the key cause-and-effect flows in a situation, your team members will pull more solidly together toward that common goal, and you will be more likely to make good decisions that avoid unintended consequences.

> **Key Insight #51:** There will always be aspects of a decision that are not captured on the diagram. The goal is to structure information that the decision maker may not be taking into account, and to drive intuition about key decision dynamics, not to provide a perfect model or simulation.

> **Key Insight #52:** The effectiveness of decision modeling should be understood as compared to the right baseline: how was this decision made in the past (usually it was unstructured, undocumented, and untracked)? Is it better now?

CONCLUSION

This section has shown how a decision model can be constructed to aid a team in choosing whether to launch a new product offering. Although the modeling process takes time and effort, each individual step is simple. What used to be "invisible" conversations are now captured visibly, in an artifact that helps everyone to be — literally — "on the same page." For projects beyond a certain complexity, where spreadsheets are the state of the art for capturing models, I've found this approach to be much more effective:

> **Key Insight #53:** It is better to organize information around the *decision* to be made instead of the *data* that drives the decision, much of which may be irrelevant.

That being said, this is a relatively new method within a relatively new field. So, make it your own: use it, extend it, write about it, and share with the emerging DI community. I look forward to hearing from you!

EXAMPLES OF DECISION INTELLIGENCE DEPLOYMENTS

We face a convergence of escalating, interlinked crises. Every day, as these crises accelerate, the capacity to address them meaningfully seems to diminish [...]. And so, we face an evolutionary moment: we either succumb to the converging catastrophes of civilisational decline, or we grasp an opportunity to transcend them by adapting new capacities and behaviours, that allow us to become more than what we were.

— Nafeez Ahmed [160]

This section presents a few additional decision model examples.

Decision Intelligence at NASA's Frontier Development Laboratory

NASA's Frontier Development Laboratory (FDL) uses DI to protect the earth from potentially hazardous asteroids and more. NASA's FDL [152] conducts AI research for space exploration and more. Several of its projects have gone beyond AI to implement DI to create "strategic decisions for the benefit of humankind" says lab director James Parr.

For instance, FDL's "Deflector Selector" project built on previous analysis regarding how to mitigate an asteroid incoming to the earth: unlike these previous projects, it determined what is the best strategic investment to make to deflect the asteroid: it used AI to explore a large number of possibilities to determine the right approach based on an asteroid's size, composition, and temporal resolution of the object [152]. Parr goes on to say that:

> *an important contribution was that, for the first time, we could say for instance that, given a known time to impact and this particular asteroid size and composition, the best approach is to use, say, a gravity tractor (or a kinetic impactor, or a nuclear device) – informing strategic investment decisions by organizations charged with planetary defense.*

Says Parr:

> *there are several additional potential DI projects within FDL, including embedding DI within space suits, helping with exploration medicine, and helping with the as much as 20-minute communications delay to Mars. We have established DI as a working language inside the lab; it is introduced to new researchers every year.*

Having implemented multiple AI and DI solutions, FDL has learned several lessons that are applicable to the community at large. One, says Parr, is that:

> *AI/DI is a team sport: the development paradigm is agile, and modular, like a Hollywood production company. Once you identify your challenge and the project workflow, you assemble specialists along it. The key is to understand all the links in the chain and to ensure all roles are filled. This allows us to build teams that deliver with a high degree of confidence.*

As a DI "lab," FDL has a distinct advantage compared to other initiatives: data quality. It is "pristine data from space, unaffected by terrestrial concerns, which gives us an amazing advantage," says Parr. This unbiased data source has allowed FDL to focus on other elements of successful AI- and DI-based project deployments, making it a pioneer in several aspects of applied AI and DI.

Utilities and Operators

New York-based Urbint uses AI and DI to enable infrastructure operators (like utility companies) to minimize risk and maximize reliability while making the tradeoffs between cost and risk transparent. Simply put, the company's ML models provide automated analysis of network assets like utility pipe, utility poles, or water mains, in order to support decisions about them. Urbint uses a three-step approach:

(1) It builds a model of the world, including data about assets and threats against them.

(2) It builds ML models that anticipate challenges to that infrastructure.

(3) It builds DI solutions that use the ML models.

In a similar pattern to the security example in Chapter 1, one of Urbint's ML models might produce a list of numbers between 0 and 1 for each asset, like a utility pole. Alone, these predictions are not actionable. How should this model be used as part of decision? Urbint follows three use case patterns:

(1) *Scoping*: In this scenario, the decision is about which assets to treat. There may be a fixed budget for doing this, in which case the decision model will treat those assets for whom the expected treatment benefit minus the expected treatment cost is the greatest. Note that "benefit" in this case might include intangible factors like safety, as well as financial ones. Or there may be a flexible budget, in which case the decision model might choose to apply the treatments that have the greatest net value, and not to treat any assets for which the expected cost exceeds the expected benefit.

(2) *Sequencing*: In some situations, regulatory or other requirements may require treating all assets in a group. Here, the ML/DI combination is used to pick the right sequence of treatment to maximize the benefit over time.

(3) *Selection*: Here, there are multiple treatments that are possible for each asset. There may be several things you can do to a gas main to extend its lifetime, for example, each with a different cost and benefit. Multiply this by 1000s of gas mains, and given the ML prediction of different treatment effectiveness for each one, there is an optimal selection and ordering of treatments.

Says Urbint Head of Product Benjamin Berry:

> *What's exciting about the combination of machine learning and decision intelligence is that often the treatment and/or ordering benefit curves are nonlinear. For example, treating 20% of the assets might produce 80% of the benefit. The question is: 'which assets fall within that 20%'?*

Looking to the future, Berry goes on to say that:

> *There are many use cases that fit this pattern, and a tremendous potential for our approach to make a difference. Adding net present value, amortization, depreciation, and lifetime analysis is an important future direction.*

Subscriber Churn Is Part of a Multi-link Decision

One of the most widespread use cases for AI is to predict the likelihood of "churn": losing a customer based on their behavior and characteristics. For instance, a customer of a magazine or a telecom that has called the billing department five times in the last month and who lives in a poor neighborhood is probably a larger risk than one who hasn't called the company for a year.

As you enter your neighborhood telecom store, you'll be asked your phone number, and if you're at risk, an alert will appear on the salesperson's screen, perhaps with a special offer for you to retain your business. The decision as to what offers to make is a DI problem. And the decision is a knife edge: making these special offers unnecessarily is costly, as is failing to retain a customer who leaves your company for another one. Multiply this decision thousands of times, and there is substantial value from getting it right.

Another decision that the telecom company might make is to enhance the bandwidth in certain neighborhoods — perhaps by enhancing the fiber optic network — in order to retain high-value and high-risk customers. This is an even more costly decision, because unnecessarily digging up a road or installing new equipment on telephone poles can cost billions of dollars annually for cable operators worldwide.

In 2014, Quantellia worked with a US cable company to combine a number of sources of information, along with multiple AI predictors (including for churn) into a decision model, to drive these capital expenditure decisions. The solution provided substantial cost savings and customer retention benefits. More recently, Toronto-based Versant Solutions is building on this work to create DI solutions that dramatically cut the time and cost of planning new networks. Says Versant's CTO Mark Zangari:

> *tasks that once took many days are now completed in a few minutes; not only is the process faster, but it also results in more efficient network designs that require fewer network elements than typical human-created designs to deliver the required performance.*

Versant's use case is similar to Urbint's, described above, in that it involves multiple choices about thousands of assets, as informed by ML. This is a widespread DI pattern used by these as well as other solutions.

Innovation Management

> *As decisions and AI are sides of the same coin, they enable growth leaders to navigate teams towards greater agility. This doesn't happen quickly. Teams reconfigure how they work collaboratively with data, technology, and across other departments. The outcome is a more resilient dynamic which adds confidence in taking bolder decisions and reduces painful opportunity costs in complex environments.*
>
> — Anand Thaker (CEO, IntelliPhi [161])

A global Fast-moving Consumer Goods (FMCG) company had thousands of innovation projects under development worldwide, each of which had the potential to generate valuable intellectual property. Its challenge was to distribute company resources to these projects so as to maximize the return on its investment (ROI).

One manager was recognized as generating the best historical ROI, relying on her experience, intuition, and the knowledge of her team [161].

However, with the advent of social media, the complexity, degree of interconnectedness, and rate of change of this task exploded. The manager suspected that better access and use of data might help her to continue meeting her ROI targets in this challenging environment. Working with Intelliphi, she conducted a series of workshops, mock decisioning scenarios, and reviews, which resulted in an AI-enabled decision support system that keeps humans in the loop. She retrained and reorganized her team and also chose to use Cloverpop to track decision making performance.

The result is a smaller portfolio of innovation projects which are producing improved ROIs. The team estimates a US $320M impact from this project over a two-year period, in the form of avoided costs plus enhancements to top-line revenues and pipeline.

A Simple Web-based Interactive Decision Model for Training Decisions

Figure 58 shows a simple decision model that you can try for yourself at the URL in this reference [39].

Figure 58. Decision Model for Value of Training.

By investing $7,097 in training that costs $100 per hour, 71 training hours can be purchased. Since the average skill level of the workforce before the investment is 3 (on a scale of 1–100), this can produce a skill-level improvement of 10 (as measured on an assessment test with a scale of 1–10) for every training hour purchased, resulting in a total predicted skills improvement score of 710. Analysis of our historical data shows that this will avoid, on average, 0 days of project delay. Project delay days cost the company, on average, $3000 each. This means that the expected benefit from the $7,097 initial investment is $0, representing a net loss of $7,097.

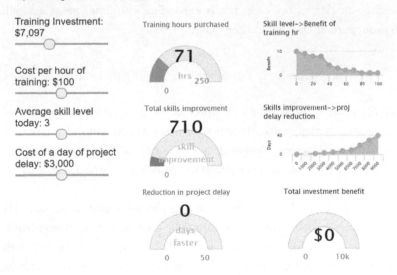

I built the original version of this model for a nuclear power plant consulting firm, who was helping its client to understand the impact of various decisions regarding training. Simply put, better-trained employees are more likely to complete projects on time, reducing costly delays and, therefore, justifying the investment in training.

But this is an overly simplistic description. As you can see in the model, the benefit of a dollar of training depends on the pre-training employee skill level. And there is a limit to the amount of skills improvement that reduces project overruns; after a certain amount, the additional benefits from better training are small.

So, in this model you can experiment with both levers on the left-hand side of the page, and you can also drag the blue dots in the graphs on the right to change these two relationships. As you make changes, the text at the top of the model changes.

Decision Intelligence for Market Decisions

Working with well-known clients like a cruise company and a large US Health Maintenance Organization (HMO), for Element Data, DI means understanding a customer or prospect's decisions, and providing data and ML capabilities that support modeling their goals and outcomes (Figure 59). Aiming, ultimately, to be "google of decisions," the company originally focused on marketing use cases but is expanding into other areas as well, such as supporting medical decision making [162].

Cable Company Sustainable Energy Generation

Many companies are facing the prospect of steep increases in the cost of energy in the coming years. In response, many are looking at alternative energy sources. However, navigating the transition to this new world contains hidden dangers, so an evidence-based modeling approach can make a big difference.

Bloomberg analyzed the decision making process surrounding how US cable operators are deciding to generate their own power — through rooftop solar arrays, wind farms, and more [163, 164]. It contracted with Quantellia to build a decision model that was used by a number of operators to integrate information from multiple sources, such as the cost of solar, the

Figure 59. Element Data's Decision Cloud Product Schematic.

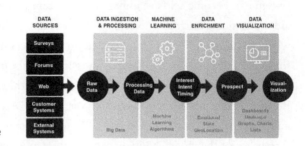

Decision Intelligence at Your Fingertips

Get the platform that:

- Enriches your data

- Identifies people in the decision state

- Gives your business the tools, insight, and data to convert those decision makers into revenue.

Source: Element data.

cost of grid energy, the rate of subscriber growth, and more, in order to align around better decisions. Key findings involved the relationship between capital power; a comparison of the effectiveness of two methods for alleviating power usage; and organizational challenges.

Decision Intelligence in Development and Conflict

In the fall of 2012, Quantellia was approached by The Carter Center [165] to study a breakthrough program in Liberia. This NGO had deployed Community Justice Advisors (CJAs) — legal paraprofessionals from local communities — to support plaintiffs and defendants as they navigated through two legal systems in Liberia: the "formal" or Monrovia-based state-run system; and the "customary" system used in more rural areas.

Since the ultimate goal of this program was peace-building, Quantellia built a systems model to explore how spending dollars on this approach, which had substantially lower infrastructure costs than more centralized programs, could help the country to "do more with less," and to move from a "vicious cycle" of conflict to a "virtuous cycle" of economic prosperity and peace.

The decision model showed that a consistent injection of aid along a number of fronts was necessary to overcome the "energy" in state space to move from one phase to another of this complex system. After this injection, the system can become self-sustaining under certain conditions. However, if the aid is not timed correctly, then the system enters a third state of "catchup," where government money is exhausted on peacekeeping, and is not available for other purposes as the democracy grows. This proof-of-concept model shows these and other dynamics, indicating that this might be the reality in Liberia; extensions include connecting the model to accurate data and cause-and-effect connections. Please see [37] for more details, Figure 60 for a screenshot of the model, and you can run the model yourself at [166].

Ted Prize winner Raj Panjabi built a decision model for another Liberian project: to demonstrate the expected impact of a health program on child mortality in advance of a meeting at the United Nations [38]. Panjabi said:

> As I was preparing my presentation for the United Nations at the Forbes 400 conference in June of 2013, I reached out to Quantellia to ask if they could help to build a decision model to analyze and illustrate the impact of Last Mile Health Front Line Health Workers on childhood mortality in Liberia. The modeling process, and subsequent video, has helped me open my eyes to my own business.

More generally, there is a recognition that international development is broken in many ways. Michael Hobbes writes:

> international development is [...] [an] [...] invasive species. Why Dertu doesn't have a vaccination clinic, why Kenyan schoolkids can't read, it's a combination of culture, politics, history, laws, infrastructure, individuals—all of a society's component parts, their harmony and their discord, working as one organism. Introducing something foreign into that system—millions in donor cash, dozens of trained personnel and equipment, U.N. Land Rovers—causes it to adapt in ways you can't predict [20].

Figure 60. System Dynamics of Aid DI Model Screen Capture.

SIMULATION OF EFFECTS OF FUNDING FOR JUSTICE ON LIBERIA'S ECONOMY*

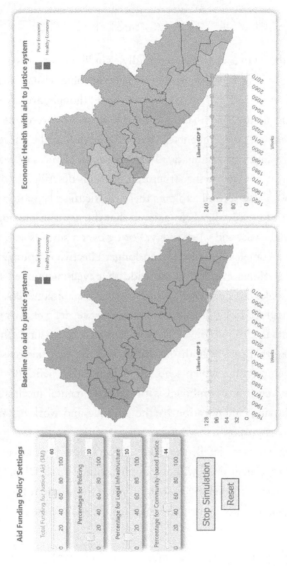

This is only a conceptual Demonstration of the simulator. The data used in the simulation is fictitious, is not intended to represent reality in any way, and should not be used as the basis for any decisions, nor should any simulation on this page be interpreted as either implicit or explicit claims about any real entities whatsoever.

Quantellia's work with The Carter Center is generously supported by a grant from the Natembea Foundation.

Although this perspective is bleak, a better understanding of complex adaptive systems, as is displayed in the early decision modeling efforts described above, is promising.

CLASSIC MISTAKES/BEST PRACTICES

If you read the above examples carefully, you'll notice some systematic patterns. Interactions between teams ... the use of a visual metaphor ... systems thinking ... and more. Not shown above, though, are the systematic *mistakes* made in decision making that DI helps to overcome. Decision making in complex environments is hard. By avoiding the most common mistake patterns, we can systematically improve our chances of reaching our goals, whether or not we use the structured methods described in other chapters of this book. This section explains these classic mistake patterns.

The mother of all mistakes is to assume that the decision making practices that worked in the past will work today. Poring over a spreadsheet, then meeting to discuss a complex situation, is no longer effective in complex environments. There is ample evidence worldwide that well-intentioned teams and organizations make decisions that lead to unintended consequences.

And, although it has tremendous potential, we are yet to harness the power of computer technology in a widespread way to find "holy grail" decisions: those that satisfy both the selfish and the selfless needs of individuals and organizations, which lead to widespread benefit. By relying on text and verbal decisions combined with invisible mental models and intuition, we are leaving collaboration by the wayside and working, more often than not, at cross-purposes.

At the next level of detail, there are some specific patterns that stand alone, providing benefit even without implementing a full DI program. For all of these patterns, it is helpful to keep in mind the shape of the CDD, with decisions leading to actions, then flowing through to outcomes.

Failing to Communicate Outcomes

A friend recently told me that she was hoping to please her new supervisor, a manager at a large industrial company. My friend, who has many decades of working in large organizations under her belt, asked for my advice as to whether she should take a number of steps that were her habit with her previous manager. I asked, "well, what are your supervisor's strategic goals for the year, because the decisions you make will either support or work at cross-purposes to them." My friend told me she didn't know, so I advised her to say at an upcoming meeting, "I want to help you as best I can, so can you share with me some of your strategic priorities for this year?"

I hesitated to include this story here because it constitutes the most fundamental aspect of leadership as it is taught in thousands of books and courses worldwide. Yet in almost every organization I have supported over the years, this most basic building block of asking "Why" has not hit home as a core element of effective decisions. For example, one team member believes we're focusing only on shareholder value ... another thinks that environmental stewardship matters too. One team member is looking for a fast return on investment ... another is willing to wait three years to be in the black in hopes of large profits ... some members of a university team tasked with reaching accreditation also wish to support its graduates in their careers, but nobody else knows that.

These stories go on and on. Every time that two team members are working toward different goals, the very real possibility exists that they will neutralize each other's efforts as they make thousands of decisions – documented and undocumented – throughout the day. And the synergies that are possible by working toward the same goal will be lost.

Now multiply this situation by the thousands of organizations of people worldwide, and you'll recognize a tremendous opportunity for better alignment and to avoid unintended consequences. This couldn't be more important in its impact on the human experience.

Documenting goals and outcomes as done using a mechanism like a CDD as described above, and then re-visiting them periodically to reinforce shared understanding, is essential to an effective decision making culture.

Miscommunications Regarding Delegated Authority

Closely related to the above point regarding the importance of understanding your superior's mental model is to understand where your own authority starts and ends.

Returning to my friend, the decision she was facing was whether to send a departmental email on behalf of her boss. Lacking a clear understanding of her supervisor's strategic goals and her own authority, she risked overstepping it. From the point of view of a CDD, this is the question of which levers are available to you and your team, and which factors should be simply taken as external constraints. Understanding whether email communication constituted a lever or an external was critical to my friend's successful interaction with her new supervisor.

A related point is that authority shifts over time. Today's levers may be tomorrow's externals and vice versa. So, it is important to periodically revisit and align this understanding with your boss and the people who report to you. A CDD can help to make this explicit.

Failing to Brainstorm Outcomes

If you don't create a safe environment to capture potential outcomes, you may miss the opportunity for synergies. You will also miss the chance to surface tacit goals, which your team members are working toward without telling you. Known in their more nefarious form as hidden agendas, these can silently destroy an organization from the inside out. Leaders should create both one-on-one meetings as well as collaborative sessions to elicit these goals.

And determining how to reach an organization's multiple goals while still meeting the needs of its employee members is arguably the most important role of a leader, a role which should be front-and-center to any initiative meant to maximize decision making power.

By brainstorming outcomes, we can obtain a rich model of goals that overcomes oversimplistic thinking that leads to unintended consequences. A recent experience: I toured Disney's EPCOT recently, including a visit to its "Under the Seas" attraction: one of the largest aquariums in the world. As with EPCOT as a whole, the aquarium was designed with two goals in mind: as an attraction, and to support research. As an organization that pays particular attention to imaginative thinking, Disney has managed to maintain both goals for Under the Seas as well as several other EPCOT initiatives, and to discover ways in which its attraction and research priorities are mutually beneficial. Indeed, blending multiple goals like entertainment, narrative, research, and more in a future-focused strategy is a strength of this organization that could benefit many others.

Confusing Proxies with Outcomes

If you add one word to your vocabulary from this book, it should be "proxy," as it applies to decisions. I introduced proxies in Chapter 1 and explored how to avoid them earlier in this chapter. Focusing on a proxy outcome closes off the possibility of other mechanisms to achieve your goal(s). For instance, if you are focused on a proxy like "customer experience" to achieve your "increase revenue" goal, you may miss other mechanisms to achieve the same goal, such as "sell to Bulgaria." If you focus on "earn more money" as a proxy for "be happier," then you might not realize that "make a new friend" might be a better way to get there.

Confusing Levers with Externals

Most decision making teams are constantly asking "what if": "what if we sell this product this year? What if we create a team to visit our congressman? What if the economy tanks?" Yet, they create unnecessary confusion by mixing decision levers (things the team can change, like the product to sell) with decision externals (things that change from the outside, like the economy).

Since one of the biggest challenges in complex decision making is that team members become confused and overwhelmed, it is important to help the team to be crisp about this distinction. We can change assumptions about externals, but not change their reality. We can create better measures about externals, but not levers (we don't measure levers, we change them ourselves).[3]

Over-reliance on Data

Data are profoundly dumb. Data can tell you that the people who took a medicine recovered faster than those who did not take it, but they can't tell you why.

— Judea Pearl [152]

Some organizations start DI projects because they (a) realize they have a lot of historical data; (b) have heard that AI can drive some value from that data; yet know that (c) the AI has to fit within a larger decision making context, which must be understood. Because the DI project is championed by the technical team in these organizations, they tend to start out the project with a focus on data: surveying, organizing, cataloging, and cleansing it. This is a tremendous mistake, and can cost millions of dollars and put a project at substantial risk.

The reason is by and large, 10% of the data hold 90% of the value. There are at least five reasons why:

(1) *Operational* data have different quality requirements than *analytical* data, yet many organizations treat them the same.

For instance, a telecommunications company I worked with used billing data (call detail records (CDRs)) both operationally and also to support decision making (such as to decide where to build new parts of its network.) For operational purposes, every call detail record mattered, because each represented billable revenue. However, to support network buildout decision making, the company only needed enough data to understand patterns and trends. This is a familiar concept to statisticians, who understand, for instance, that polling data can be used effectively to predict an election. But you'd be surprised how many organizations say "the decision is only as good as the data," by which they mean that they must do the equivalent of polling every voter. This is not necessary for many use cases.

This point deserves reiteration: *data management is the "hidden stepchild" of many projects*: cleansing, joining, or processing giga- or terabytes is a daunting task, and is usually vastly underestimated. A banking friend of mind said, indeed, that "every project we've worked on has significant data challenges." To build a good model, substantial data cleansing is often not needed. Though note: to *use* that model effectively you'll often be feeding operational data into it, so the operational cleansing challenge remains.

Another example: we built an intrusion detection system for a security company recently. To build a model that could detect intrusion patterns, the data did not have to be cleansed or analyzed to any great extent. But now the model must be deployed into production: if the data about system behavior that goes into the model has a systematic bias, then we may create a lot of false alarms or perhaps miss intrusions that we should have caught.

(2) When you "connect the dots" between data and benefit (e.g. revenue), *some data fields have a big impact, and some not so much.* So, for instance, the color of your competitor's product may not turn out to matter much to your competitive position. But their price does. This is an obvious example, but there are many not-so-obvious ones as well. The principal here is that *knowledge of how the data combines with decisions to impact business objectives is a valuable resource to identify the important data.*

Many organizations stovepipe their data people, so that they don't have access to this bigger picture, and ask their teams to "just make it all as clean as you can." This can be a tremendous waste of resources. For instance, I worked with one organization that spent 18 months trying to find keys to join about a hundred tables reflecting customer data. When we did a preliminary analysis for this organization, we learned that a join between just two tables would give them much of the insight that they required.

(3) Decisions are not made of just data, but they are also based on human expertise, things you may not have thought yet to measure, and intangible factors (as studied by value network analysis (VNA) [167]) like reputation and brand. For this reason, looking to data as the sole basis for decision support is a bit like looking for your keys under the lamppost. Again, if we work backward from business outcomes using a DI approach, we often find that the most valuable information needed to support that decision is not in existing data stores.

(4) In many environments, there are no data for your situation, because they are brand-new. Here, we need to generate "data from the future" [27, 119] or use transfer learning [29].

(5) In many organizations, as described in Chapter 3, feedback effects ultimately dominate, so detailed data information is less important [168].

Allowing Perfection to be the Enemy of the "Better"

As described earlier in this chapter, some misunderstand the purpose of decision modeling as to be creating a completely accurate model of the situation, which is impossible. "Moving the needle" of improved understanding and alignment by stakeholders, even if only by a bit, can have tremendous value.

Expecting Consensus

No two people can ever think identically about the same decision, even if the CDD is drawn in great detail. Subconscious information and intuition are both extremely valuable and also can't be easily captured. For this reason, it is important to have realistic expectations. A decision modeling exercise still requires a responsible party to have the authority to make the decision, as covered more below.

Responsibility without Corresponding Authority and Vice Versa

If you will be held responsible for certain outcomes, you must be given the authority to affect the levers that impact those outcomes. Anything else is a recipe for insanity [169]. Conversely, if you or your team have the authority to change things but are not held responsible for the outcomes, this is a recipe for a different kind of disaster. Called "moral hazard" in economics [170], this pattern underlies some of the biggest decision fails of history, including the 2008 Global Financial Crisis [171].

I have faced many situations where I am responsible for a decision, yet others wish to remove my authority. They go beyond the suggestion to insistence, forcing me to defend every detail of my rationale, or my decision will not be accepted.

While it is of course good to challenge decision rationale to some degree, there will always remain some element of my own unconscious knowledge that goes into decision making that I cannot defend verbally. Assuming otherwise means we are falling for the fallacy that all knowledge can be made conscious and explicit. As long as I am responsible for the outcomes of my decisions, I must be allowed to select the levers (make the choices), whether or not I can explicitly explain my rationale. If others are willing to take on responsibility, then this tension is removed because we are now relying on their intuition, not mine.

Another way to think of responsibility and authority is that they sit in a triad with information, as shown in Figure 61. These three elements must be in balance: without adequate information I will use my authority to make bad decisions; those with information and no authority nor responsibility may attempt to usurp the situation with negative consequences; responsibility without information is another recipe for insanity. And "Information"

Figure 61. Balancing Responsibility, Authority, and Information.

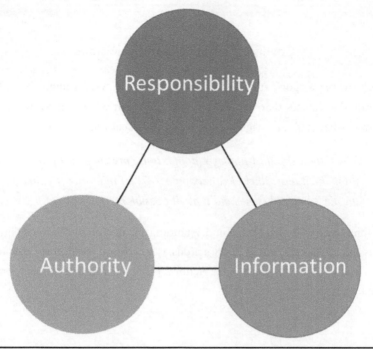

here represents more than just data: it is the full analysis that comes from collaboration, a good decision model, and more. The better my information sources, the more effective my decisions.

Assuming That Decision Modeling Requires a Sophisticated Technical Background

Anyone can build a decision model. In fact, everyone does: throughout your day, you're imagining how your choices will play out over time.

There are forces at play that will make you feel that you are not smart enough nor knowledgeable enough about AI, data, evidence, and more to participate in a decision making exercise. This is not true. Don't allow technical jargon to fill a room: honor and respect your technicians but insist that communication be understandable by everyone. Even within technology, this is a shifting playing field, as democratized AI systems that can be used by non-specialists are emerging. You can drive a car without understanding the

carburetor, and you can use advanced technology effectively without understanding how it works.

Confusing Predictions with Decisions

You're at the airport, running for the gate. An AI system might be able to
tell you the chances that you'll miss your flight. But what you really want to
know is what to do, the right *action* based on a decision.

> *What flight should I book to (a) maximize my chances of making it;*
> *(b) make it most likely I can fly on a 787; (c) minimize my time in*
> *the air; (d) avoid Cleveland if at all possible?*

To think clearly in this space, understanding the distinction between predictions and decisions that lead to actions is important. Initiatives like those
described in "Data to Knowledge Action" [172] indicate the growing understanding of this distinction.

NOTES

1. Remember that outcomes are what you measure (like customer experience), and
goals are the values of outcomes you'll consider "good" (like customer experience
over 75% on a particular survey).

2. The "how" here is a "how would you measure it", not a "how would you accom-
plish it" meaning of the word "how", so not part of the why/how chain mechanism.
Yes, it's confusing: English as a language isn't quite up to this.

3. See https://youtu.be/BzigRlLAjPE?t=815 [213] for a decision model that includes
both an external — the interest rate — and several levers (in yellow).

CHAPTER 5

THE POWER OF THE DECISION MODEL FRAMEWORK

There are two sources of learning: learning from reflecting on the past, and learning from sensing and actualizing emerging future possibilities.

> — Otto Sharma, reflections upon returning from a discussion with the Dalai Lama [173].

The best way to predict the future is to create it.

> — Dennis Gabor [174]

Through the simple step of making a decision visible through a causal decision diagram (CDD) or similar diagram, and by using a structured decision making process like decision intelligence (DI), an explosion of new approaches to solving complex problems emerges. Figure 62 illustrates a few of them. Space doesn't allow for detailed descriptions of each one, so the following sections give brief explanations and pointers.

DI AS A MECHANISM FOR HUMAN/MACHINE COLLABORATION/INTELLIGENCE AUGMENTATION (IA)

Humans are good at drawing decision diagrams, computers (despite AI hype) are not: they simply don't understand how the world works in any reliable way. Computers are, however, good at:

• providing tools to help draw decision diagrams;

Figure 62. Decision Intelligence (DI) Has Implications for Many Domains.

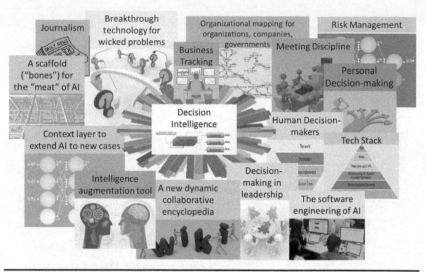

- assembling qualitative and quantitative flows in the CDD into an interactive simulation;

- searching for the decisions that lead to the best outcomes; and

- creating interactive and immersive game-like environments that help to drive human intuition regarding complex situations.

For these reasons, a CDD is a mechanism for unifying human and computer expertise. IA was covered in more detail in Chapter 3.

DI FOR EDUCATION

DI embodies the critical thinking capabilities most needed by global citizens in the twenty-first century, and can form the basis for educational programs. Video games like World of Warcraft are already teaching children to interact collaboratively within complex simulated worlds; the next step is for children to create their own CDDs and simulations of their own world.

DI AS A TOOL TO SUPPORT DECISION MAKING AND ORGANIZATIONAL INFLUENCE MAPPING IN ORGANIZATIONS/COMPANIES AND GOVERNMENTS

The CDD approach is particularly valuable in organizations that wish to work hand-in-hand with technology to make decisions informed by data and AI.

One example is a California university where student learning outcomes are defined in each course, each academic degree program, and at the institutional level (where the definition explains what every graduate should demonstrate). Valerie Landau created a DI-related assessment method that helps universities through the accreditation process that facilitates an effective cycle of continuous improvement in teaching and learning and earns commendation from accreditors. It also creates an institutional portfolio with links from each learning outcome to samples of student work that demonstrate those competencies. It makes the interactions "live" through an interactive software portal, which is illustrated in Figure 63.

Landau created www.aimosaic.com to build on this work by helping for-profit and nonprofit organizations and policy initiatives to draw maps that help them understand these connections of the outcomes at different levels.

Figure 63. A Visualization that Links Courses, Programs, and University Learning Outcomes.

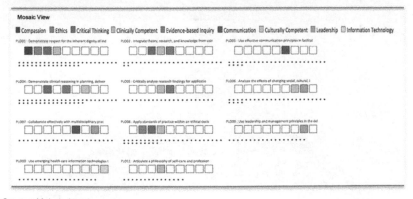

Source: Valerie Landau.

DI AS THE TECHNOLOGY THAT GLUES THE TECH STACK TO THE HUMAN STACK

Technology adds several new sources of information to those that humans use to make decisions. These include data, reports, and visualizations that summarize that data, models (AI and more) that enhance that data, and software applications that consolidate this information into a form in which it can be readily consumed by humans.

This "technology stack" must meet what we might call the "reality stack" of human decision makers, working within a team to make choices, and implementing them in an organization in such a way that it impacts stakeholders and, ultimately, the world at large, as shown in Figure 64.

Central to the technology stack are flows of *code* and *data*. Central to the reality stack are flows of *causation,* which we can think of as the events that are set in motion by actions taken by humans based on their decisions. These two worlds – technology and reality – meet at a simple interface: the

Figure 64. The "Reality Stack" Shows How Technology Supports Human Decision Makers.

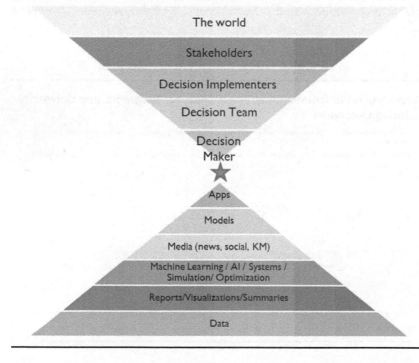

decision. DI is driving the development of increasingly powerful, yet simple-to-use, applications and methodologies at the point marked with the star, where technology supports human decision makers in the most intuitive way possible.

DI AS THE CORE OF SOFTWARE THAT IS BASED ON WORLD MODELS

There are two kinds of software systems: those that — like word processors — act as tools, and those that simulate the world. An increasing number of software applications today are in the latter category. For instance, a project management system contains simulated tasks and human resources.

Although there are certainly software systems that implement and support such world model-based decisions, until now there has been no commonality from one to the next. Much like using the same kind of blueprints for all buildings, a shared representational scheme creates an explosion of new possibilities [175].

DI AS A LEADERSHIP AND MANAGEMENT DISCIPLINE

A CDD illustrates a critical difference between the processes of gathering information regarding a decision — which results in the diagram — and making that decision itself. Leaders are often caught in a dilemma between the need to solicit advice and the need to move forward decisively. The diagram illustrates one solution: advisors are for providing information, but not for choosing the levers; these represent choices that require information which typically goes beyond what can be captured in the diagram, because it is based on the unconscious — but highly rational — knowledge of the decision maker, as was described in more detail in Chapter 4.

Decision diagrams also make visual any explicit concepts like *ideology, assumption, proxy goal, authority, responsibility, information,* and more [176]. My experience looking at my own business through this new lens makes me suspect that the topic of leadership through a DI lens is worth an entire book in itself!

Figure 65. DI Can Identify and Manage Systematic Risks.

GFC
2008 Global Financial Crisis
Complex causal network of derivatives and underwriting created a single point of failure in the global financial system.

WW 1
World War I
Due to a complex network of treaties and alliances, a single assassination snowballed into global conflict.

Apollo 13
1970 Apollo 13 moon mission
An oxygen tank was dropped during its fabrication – at the time, a harmless error. But downstream dependencies caused the tank to rupture in space seven years later.

Carillion
2018 Failure of Carillion
Income/Debt fell, triggering the need for more debt in an unconstrained feedback loop.

Source: www.theriskframework.com.

DI AS A RISK MANAGEMENT FRAMEWORK

By mapping decisions through a systems diagram, individual risks which are prone to becoming systemic risks can be detected and monitored, as illustrated in Figure 65. The website www.theriskframework.com offers DI-based risk analysis solutions, with a focus on commercial credit risk.

DI AS AN ANALYSIS FRAMEWORK FOR AI ETHICS AND RESPONSIBILITY

Closely related to risk analysis is the use of DI to support ethical and responsible AI. An expert in this arena is Reid Blackman, CEO of ethics consultancy Virtue, which offers organizational and new technology (including AI) risk and ethics consulting. Reid points out that AI ethics goes considerably beyond bias, which is receiving the greatest attention today. He breaks down ethical risk into the following six categories:

(1) physical mental harm: death or addiction;

(2) privacy;

(3) trust and respect;

(4) relationships and social cohesion;

(5) fairness and justice; and

(6) unintended consequences.

DI has the greatest impact on #6: both for avoiding negative as well as for maximizing positive consequences [117]. Automated solutions like DI create "action-at-a-distance," separating actors from their consequences. Formally called *moral hazard* [177], this kind of risk grows with increasing automation, and must be understood and managed. By providing a visual map of the consequences of a decision, DI supports this process. Expert consultancies like Virtue are also essential.

DI AS A SOFTWARE ENGINEERING DISCIPLINE FOR AI

I showed how AI systems fit into a CDD in Chapter 2. Drawing the CDD collaboratively is a good step for any AI project, to align the expectations of decision makers with the goal of the AI team.

> **Key Insight #54:** A CDD is a good way to draw the requirements for many machine learning projects, because it shows how the ML model(s) interact with the rest of the organization to drive outcomes with value.

DI AS A CONTEXT LAYER THAT EXTENDS AI TO NEW USE CASES

Most current AI systems are restricted to predictive analytics, classification natural language processing (NLP), and pattern recognition. As I showed in Chapter 2, DI is a structured way to inject AI models into systems that help users to understand: "If I take this action, what will be the outcome," instead of simple question answering or "thing labeling" [178].

DI AS A BREAKTHROUGH TECHNOLOGY TO SOLVE "WICKED" PROBLEMS

The hard problems we face as a species – climate change, conflict, poverty, inequality, democracy, and more – require multi-link solutions. As

I described above, DI goes considerably beyond individual existing technologies in this regard: they must be combined to solve the hard problems.

DI AS A WAY OF BETTER UNDERSTANDING PERSONAL DECISIONS: INDIVIDUALLY AND WITHIN ORGANIZATIONS

Even in situations where it doesn't make sense to go to the trouble of drawing a CDD or building an automated decision simulator, simply understanding the elements of a decision in a structured way can improve critical thinking.

DI AS A MEETING DISCIPLINE

A few years back I worked with a team to teach DI to a school board of directors in making difficult decisions in the face of criminal allegations against a member of their faculty. We taught them how to structure decision making conversations, to argue about the decision structure rather than against each other. Through understanding the CCD, and then working through the decision elements one at a time, the board was able to achieve a consensus that they told me would otherwise not have been possible.

DI AS A GENERATIVE MODEL FOR CHATBOTS SUPPORTING DECISION MAKING

Many governments and organizations are now offering AI-based chat systems that answer basic questions and help users fill in forms. Moving forward, a number of researchers are beginning to explore how a chatbot equipped with a decision model can be used to guide such conversations. This becomes particularly exciting when the decision model is dynamically created by a Wikipedia-like curating crowd.

DI AS THE BASIS FOR A NEW FORM OF DYNAMIC "WIKIPEDIA"

Current information resources are static, and provide pieces of decision models: a fact here, a prediction there, a cause-and-effect link here.

Assembling this piecemeal information into coherent models — either static graphics or dynamic simulations — is the inevitable next step.

DI AS A FOUNDATION FOR JOURNALISM IN AN AGE OF COMPLEXITY

Ideally, the job of a responsible journalist is to educate us regarding the events of the day in such a way that we can make informed decisions about our lives and votes. When events are complex, journalism that focuses on only linear stories fails us.

Dr Nafeez Masada Ahmed is creating a new paradigm that communicates interdependent links and nonlinear effects including vicious and virtuous cycles. Ahmed says, "We need to go back to each of [the global] crises, understand how they work, and understand fundamentally how they are interconnected." His documentary film, called *The Crisis of Civilization*, illustrates his approach [179].

Speaking to the solution, Ahmed points to how we understand interdependencies:

> *Once we recognize there's a problem in the way that information systems are structured, then you ask 'why?' It turns out that information systems are not structured to comprehend reality. If that's the case, then the simple solution is how do you restructure to comprehend reality and then engage with it? [180]*

Ahmed points out, however, that "there is no incentive structure today to create multidisciplinary journalism; if it is happening here and there, then that is only by accident. To change this, we must overcome deeply entrenched institutional patterns: the purpose of journalism by and large is not to tell the truth, but rather to produce information so that companies can make money" [180].

Shining a light at a level of reality that cuts through these stories to the underlying interdependencies is a core goal of decision intelligence. However, as Ahmed explains, there are considerable forces preventing this kind of clarity in journalism. I hope that this book inspires those in a position to make an impact to support efforts like Ahmed's [181].

Just as data visualization plays an important role in journalism today, decision and complex systems visualization will become increasingly important in the future. Journalism platforms should also be more social and collaborative, to support documentation of multiple opinions about interdependent effects and to lead to better consensus.

DI AS A BUSINESS TRACKING DISCIPLINE

Most businesses review basic numbers, such as revenues, costs, and cash flow, on a regular basis, then make tactical and strategic decisions. Most of the time, the review is based on historical or current numbers, and the task of thinking about how decisions will interact with the future is left as an exercise that happens inside the decision makers' heads. We can do much better.

It is now standard practice for many professionals who create complex artifacts — from airline pilots to engineers building a bridge — to run computer simulations. DI brings this simulation discipline to the board room, and running a forward model will become standard practice. Serial entrepreneur Jim Casart says:

> I see DI as the basis for a new kind of business management, where the monthly meeting is forward-looking and simulation-based instead of just summarizing backward-looking numbers. There's a reason why a car's rear-view mirror is smaller than its windshield. [19]

DI FOR GOVERNMENT PLANNING

As the world changes more rapidly, a government's ability to plan for the future is a key capability. This past summer, the Orlando Economic Partnership invited Kedge — a foresight consultancy that uses many of the principles described in this book — to facilitate a new strategic transformation for the city of Orlando. This followed Kedge's history as the official provider of foresight development inside Walt Disney International across 23 countries since 2012.

The project involved 250 stakeholders across the Central Florida region, including Disney, and its final outcome was presented at EPCOT in late 2018 in what is now called "Launch To Tomorrow (LTT)."

Kedge's Frank Spencer says:

> the LTT project revealed a new direction for Central Florida – to realize Walt's original dream of EPCOT (Experimental Prototype Community of Tomorrow)! Not a theme park, as it ended up becoming, but as an actual city that promotes broad-based prosperity through social entrepreneurship, technology, widespread inclusion, and participatory foresight.

The practical actions to make that vision a reality are now well under way. Kedge is now partnering with the Orlando Economic Partnership's Leadership Orlando and Foundation for the Future to train community leaders to create the future using Strategic Foresight and action-oriented Futures Thinking techniques. Integrating AI and data are on the LTT road map.

DI FOR INTELLIGENCE ANALYSIS

As illustrated in Figure 66 [182] a widespread lens through which the benefit of national intelligence collection and analysis is viewed is in providing "decision advantage" in a conflict situation. For instance, CIA officer N. John MacGaffin and defense expert Peter C. Oleson say: "[...] the 1962 Cuba missile crisis is a good example of intelligence giving decision advantage to President Kennedy despite the fact that the latest National Intelligence Estimate discounted the possibility of Khrushchev placing missiles on the island. Tipped by SIGINT and some disturbing HUMINT reports, a U-2 spy plane mission collected photography revealing the existence of offensive missiles on the island, without the Soviets knowing about the discovery." [183]

And, more recently, senator Jack Reed emphasized the United States' increasing disadvantage in this realm:

> [China] is undertaking a significant national investment in artificial intelligence and quantum computing that is dwarfing anything that the administration is proposing or suggesting [...] if artificial

Figure 66. How Intelligence Collection, Integration, and Analysis Lead to Decision Advantage.

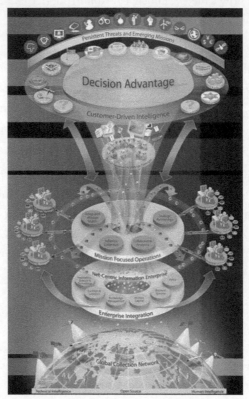

Source: ODNI.

intelligence has even half of the benefits that its promoters claim, it is going to be extraordinarily disruptive [...] where is our national Manhattan program for AI and quantum computing that will match the Chinese? [...] [The Chinese] are generating their own intellectual property at a rate that could be disruptive and we are not matching that. [184]

A comprehensive DI program may represent an opportunity for the United States to catch up on the world stage, leapfrogging current AI initiatives to the next level of sophistication.

CHAPTER 6

LOOKING TO THE FUTURE

Despite the tremendous problems we face, our world of expanding complexity is not a sign that we are collapsing, but is really an indication that we are growing.
— Frank Spencer, Kedge/The Futures School [185]

There's a great big, beautiful tomorrow, shining at the end of every day. There's a great big beautiful tomorrow. And tomorrow's just a dream away.
— Walt Disney, *Carousel of Progress* [186]

To improve is to change; so to be perfect is to have changed often.
— Winston Churchill [187]

Many of the great advancements of the industrial revolution can be traced back to *quality* — total quality management (TQM), business process management (BPM), and a cluster of related disciplines can be viewed as core to major advancements in the twenty-first century, with their early and/or late adoption driving events no less than the fate of the United States vs Japanese automobile markets, and much more [188]. Core to these developments were structured methods to understand processes and flow of goods and human resources.

As we move forward into the knowledge-based economy of the twenty-first century, the next frontier of mapping and structured understanding is the *Decision*: an event — whether performed by man or machine — that characterizes the thought process around how actions lead to outcomes. Improving those decisions, through better alignment, collaboration, and continuous improvement, will define the success of this next phase in human existence.

This chapter looks forward into the future of Decision Intelligence (DI), to give you a flavor of some of the new initiatives that are growing from this foundational new discipline.

NEW IDEAS, NEW DI EVANGELISTS

The endeavor described in this book is ambitious: creating as it does a new context for technology, science, and everyday people to contribute to important solutions. It is also a very young field. Like a boisterous toddler, is new enough that those of us evangelizing the field (and that includes you, if you've read this far) still have an opportunity for great influence; yet it is mature enough we can be sure it's real, and a lot of fun, if a bit chaotic and unformed.

As I write these words in California, I have just now finished an interview with yet another new DI practitioner acquaintance. His company was started a few years back based on some of mine and Mark Zangari's early writings. And yesterday I met another employee of a major platform company, who tells me he's evangelizing DI company-wide. Yesterday I also heard about a new entity called the Global Challenges Collaboration (GCC) [189], with substantial overlap to the ideas here.

As these relationships build every day, it becomes increasingly obvious how unbounded the field of DI is, which explains its historical separation into multiple disciplines. But allowing the entropy to persist leaves a huge opportunity on the table: it is up to you and me to develop a framework for reunifying these disciplines to solve the hardest problems.

So where will DI go next? Will it, as discussed in Chapter 3, end up reconstituting Cybernetics? Is it realistic to create such a large and interdisciplinary field? When I started this work, these were serious questions for me. But over the years, and while writing this book, I have come to believe that the story introduced here is an inevitable and important development in the twenty-first century.

THE HEADWIND OF DISRUPTION

DI is emerging through a paradigm shift. It is facing a headwind, within a millennial-length trend of how people see themselves in relation to nature.

Only in recent times have we moved beyond a view of humans on a pedestal somehow able to manifest "pure thought," qualitatively different from the world in which we live. With the advent of behavioral economics, the movement from symbolic to sub-symbolic AI and statistics — the science of uncertainty — we realize that we are as imperfect as the rest of the things.

The next step, says Google Cloud's Chief Decision Scientist Cassie Kozyrkov [15], is

> *to build man back up, to accept that we are imperfect, and to build tools that make us better. Those mathematical tools come from data science, and their effectiveness depends on us designing them in light of our animal nature, not in ignorance of it.*

So far, these tools have not been on this philosophical ride. Kozyrkov points to cross-field disdain as a barrier to interdisciplinary work.

> **Key Insight #55:** Working upstream against specialization requires a shift in the often tacit understanding that to be smarter we must become more specialized: a position that upon examination is obviously flawed, yet represents a deeply entrenched belief system, at least as far as academia and research is concerned. Another benefit of re-integration of knowledge is the increased benefit of understanding (as opposed to being frustrated and paralyzed by) the results of the rapidly increasing complexity.

Yet the nature of the problems we face demands such an interdisciplinary, interdependent understanding: a view with a deep trunk and root, going back at least half a century.

Kozyrkov says that there may be "diminishing returns to improving life through amassing more and more of the same type of knowledge; eventually real breakthroughs might require us to think outside boxes and between them, radically synthesizing knowledge by exploring bridges between isolated academic disciplines."

> **Key Insight #56:** Indeed, we have enough *answers* today in many realms, yet not enough knowledge of the results of *actions* based on those answers. We have lost the ability to stitch the answers together to see how an action taken today leads to an outcome tomorrow.

This is the next most important revolution – neither purely scientific nor technological; it is a hybrid that allows us to use the answers in the most valuable way for the benefit of humanity.

DI is also arguably an important element of World Economic Forum Klaus Schwab's Fourth Industrial Revolution, in which exponential technologies like the Internet of Things, AI, quantum computing, and nanotechnology are changing business models and impacting policy worldwide [190].

DI is galloping forward in a hundred directions at once. This chapter describes a few new DI-related initiatives that have crossed my radar. I briefly describe the emerging DI ecosystem of companies and other organizations, new DI-related narratives in fiction, and DI-related work in disability support and a shift to democracy as we know it.

THE DI ECOSYSTEM TODAY AND TOMORROW

In my work with technologists, politicians, economists, and more, I observe that tech is most ready for radical system change. The popularity of blockchain, for instance, represents this community's recognition of the need for a massive shift in how we think about wealth. Education, in contrast, they want to 'fix education' instead of realizing that the paradigm is broken. Tech is limited in its perspective though, so its disruptive intentions need to be informed by connections to these other fields.

– Nora Bateson [65]

This book has, by necessity, explored only a part of DI, and has a technology bias. This is only an artifact of my own experience, and should not be taken as reflecting the focus – descriptive or prescriptive – of the field going forward.

Not only is my own lens technology-focused, but so is only a corner of the wider ecosystem that I know about. Companies that have indicated to me at one time or another that they are in the DI ecosystem include FICO, DNV-GL, Quantellia, Satavia, Prowler.io, DecisionCloud, PowerNoodle, Sympatico, eHealthAnalytics, gongos, busigence, EvenClever, PureTech, SAP, OpsPro, infoharvest, and absolutdata.

Consulting company Kedge/The Futures School's approach to "Wicked Opportunities" is a particularly strong articulation of this ecosystem's vision:

Several years ago we trademarked "Wicked Opportunities," a concept that we have been working with for quite some time. This phrase is the opposite of Wicked Problems, the idea that most problems that we deal with today are so complex that when we attempt to solve them, we create three or more new problems.

Our old way of thinking, cemented in Industrial Age practices such as siloing, short-term ROI and the efficiency movement effectively vilified complexity as the enemy of humanity. In reality, complexity is the natural order of growth and maturity in evolutionary systems. It isn't complexity that's the enemy − it's our outdated mindsets and processes.

Yes, Wicked Problems are certainly complex, multiplying and often dangerous. But what if we are exacerbating them, amplifying them − even creating them − through siloed fields and knowledge?

What if we are missing the opportunities offered through convergence, meshing and the maturing landscape of complex adaptive systems? What if our wicked problems are actually hidden wicked (complex) opportunities? [1]

If the above companies might be considered "core" DI firms, there is a much larger ecosystem of surrounding companies that offer decision support, systems modeling, and business intelligence software and/or services, all of which make valuable contributions to this ecosystem.

One example is the Long Now Foundation based in San Francisco. From its mission statement, the Foundation "[...] hopes to provide a counterpoint to today's accelerating culture and help make long-term thinking more common. We hope to foster responsibility in the framework of the next 10,000 years" [191]. With a board that includes tech visionaries like Danny Hillis (of Connection Machine fame), Global Business School network founder Steward Brand, and *Wired* magazine cofounder Kevin Kelly, the Foundation's mission reflects a growing movement amongst senior Silicon Valley technologists to move to a "next level."

Another example is Nicole Helmer who runs a decision intelligence team within enterprise technology vendor SAP. Her group's charter is to help startup companies as well as "intrapreneurial" groups within SAP to make evidence-based decisions to pivot repeatedly toward success. Although the data sets used by her organizations contain only thousands of rows, and so might be considered "small" instead of "big data," the decisions that they support have considerable value. For this reason, human expertise must work hand-in-hand with data, bridging the qualitative to the quantitative, combining the best of both worlds: intuition from founders and empirical evidence from the search for product/market fit.

For Helmer, the use of the name "decision intelligence" helps to place an emphasis on her team's desired outcome – to make a good decision – as opposed to a particular method. Helmer says,

> *Decision intelligence says I can use the simplest method available to make the best possible decision. That could mean using a spreadsheet, machine learning, or some other method. By focusing on the decision instead of the particular technology, I have maximum latitude to pick the right tool for each task.*

Helmer goes on to say that the focus on the decision helps her communicate effectively with stakeholders:

> *If I am talking with a new internal or external client, it's hard for me to explain the kinds of problems that data scientists can solve. Letting them know that we are using data to make a decision to start with, rather than AI or ML, helps me to communicate effectively based on what people already know. [192]*

EMERGING DATA SCIENTIST SPECIALIST ROLES

As shown in Figure 67, data science (including ML and AI) is transitioning into widespread commercial usage in a pattern that is reminiscent of the path followed by computer science in the past.

Helmer's work with many startup organizations has also given her a unique perspective on emerging roles as ML/AI/data science makes this transition. "Data science," says Helmer, "is in a position that computer science used to hold. These days we call ourselves front-end coders, full-stack coders, and more, but not 'computer scientists'. The fields have specialized, and that's happening within the data science world too. We are starting to see job postings for 'machine learning engineer', 'decision intelligence analyst', and 'data science engineer' which is reflecting this specialization.

Figure 67. Data Science Is Transitioning into a Commercialization Phase, Much as Computer Science Transitioned in the Past. This Is Driving a Need for New Specialized Roles.

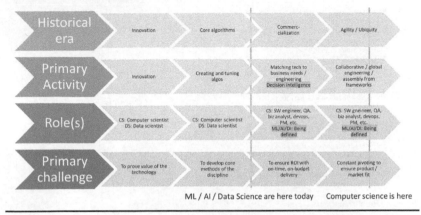

ML / AI / Data Science are here today   Computer science is here

Figure 68. The Emerging "Agile AI" Lifecycle, Compared to the Well-established Software Engineering Lifecycle.

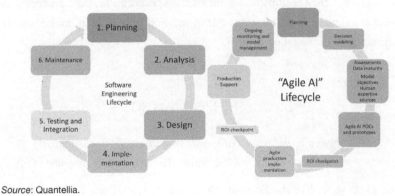

Source: Quantellia.

The skills within these emerging subfields are very different: one person might know how to set up ETL [extract/transform/load of data streams], and another may have never even heard of it."

One way to express these roles is to relate them to a "software engineering lifecycle" diagram that has been around for many years, and is shown on the left-hand side of Figure 68. Quantellia's related "Agile AI lifecycle" is shown on the right.

Figure 69. New Specialist Roles Driven by AI/ML/DI as It Transitions into More Widespread Use.

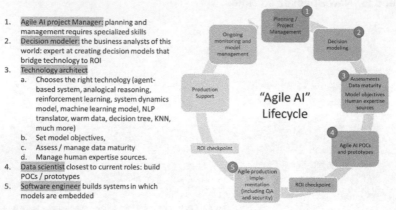

1. Agile AI project Manager: planning and management requires specialized skills
2. Decision modeler: the business analysts of this world: expert at creating decision models that bridge technology to ROI
3. Technology architect
   a. Chooses the right technology (agent-based system, analogical reasoning, reinforcement learning, system dynamics model, machine learning model, NLP translator, warm data, decision tree, KNN, much more)
   b. Set model objectives,
   c. Assess / manage data maturity
   d. Manage human expertise sources.
4. Data scientist closest to current roles: build POCs / prototypes
5. Software engineer builds systems in which models are embedded

Source: Quantellia.

Associated with some of the steps on the right-hand side of Figure 68 are new emerging roles, shown in Figure 69. Not all projects will require all of these roles, but they do illustrate some of the specialties that are emerging as AI/ML transitions into commercialization, and which will make up an important part of the DI ecosystem.

DI AND THE NEW MYTHOS

In the beginning the power of words must have seemed magical [...]
— Alan Watts, *The Wisdom of Insecurity* [24]

When great shifts like the DI re-synthesis happen, they are reflected in and catalyzed by the stories we tell ourselves.

Until now, most great stories — from Homer to Disney's Mulan — are about the "hero's journey": we celebrate an individual protagonist who explores a new world, encounters obstacles, and returns triumphant.

This narrative is increasingly falling short. We need, instead, stories that tell of unintended consequences, complex systems, collaboration, and actions that lead to a chain of events in space and in time — effectively we need a new set of archetypes which science fiction author (and former motion picture executive and Disney employee) PJ Manney calls "the new Mythos."

Her novels are, in part, about the unintended consequences of technology, which are systematically overlooked.

Manney explains:

> *scientists don't benefit from talking much about possible unintended consequences of their work, which seeds doubt amongst funding agencies. But technology does create negative as well as positive effects, and it is critical that we embrace the effort to understand them. We must look at technology through an empathetic lens. It is one thing to build things in isolation; it is quite another to imagine being in the shoes of users and understanding the chains of events that technology sets in motion.*

I visited Disney World recently, where I was struck by Walt Disney's future-focused thinking: his EPCOT vision ("Experimental Prototype City of Tomorrow") was, sadly, never realized, but was intended to be never finished. EPCOT was a continuation of Disney's path from short cartoons, through features, then theme parks, to the next level of intended impact on urban planning and, ultimately, society as a whole. The common theme in Disney's history is narrative, along with increasing immersion in it. And his goal was to catalyze the widespread shifts needed to take us to a new place. And the Disney corporation's choice of a Buckminster-Fuller-inspired Spaceship Earth at the opening to EPCOT indicates a continuation of the themes of this book.

Manney explains another emerging story theme that goes, "when we use logic, we make bad decisions." The Terminator backstory was influenced by the movie *Colossus: the Forbin Project*, where an evil Artificial General Intelligence (AGI) concludes that humans are stupid, runs logic to its conclusion, and creates havoc. AGIs in movies like this one, says Manney, are allegories for human fears of "organizational robots," specifically our loss of control over governments and military organizations. These stories reflect a sense of futility; we can't possibly understand nor control increasing societal complexity. But there is another narrative: that this is only a transient state, as we develop new tools like DI to help.

"If we are to survive," says Manney, "we must be able to start employing larger contexts and to understand how we fit into them [...] this is not about having to give away your things [...] it is not collectivism. It is simply being more thoughtful, and writing about the group dynamics of worlds, and to understand a greater number of moving parts" [193].

THE HUMAN ELEMENT

There is always a lot of input and output. The input and the output happen in every second, and we should learn how to look at life as streams of being, and not as separate entities. This is a very profound teaching of the Buddha.

— Thich Nhat Hanh [194]

Increasingly human perception, response and behavior is becoming digitized. The ultimate promise of AI/ML is to utilize this data to help us become our better selves, the ultimate betrayal is to exploit our psychology.

— Charles Davis, CTO/Cofounder ElementData [124]

Progress in new endeavors like DI must be accompanied by new insights within individuals. Kathia Castro Laszlo writes:

we will not be living better lives if we do not transform ourselves, our lifestyles, choices and priorities [...] Systems being involves embodying a new consciousness, an expanded sense of self, a recognition that we cannot survive alone, that a future that works for humanity needs also to work for other species and the planet. [...] This is the wisdom of many indigenous cultures [...] part of the heritage that we have forgotten, and we are in the process of recovering [...] Systems being and systems living brings it all together: linking head, heart and hands [195].

Indeed, many spiritual traditions embody the following insight.

Key Insight #57: The greatest wisdom about the future begins by entering the present moment.

AI, DI, AND THE LAW

Legal and policy decisions are some of the most impactful on societies worldwide. The legal profession is changing substantially in response to AI, in particular natural language processing (NLP), which supports analysis and creation of legal documents such as contracts, thereby automating many tasks in the legal profession. James A. Sherer, a partner in the New York office of BakerHostetler LLP, says: "[...] AI is [...] impacting current attorney practice in four discrete areas: (1) document review in e-discovery ("predictive coding" or technology-assisted review), (2) contract due diligence review in corporate transactions, (3) third-party legal research products in multiple practice areas, and (4) time entry and matter analysis" [8].

Another perspective comes from Michele Colucci, a Silicon-valley based legal technology entrepreneur and CEO of Justiquity.com. Figure 70 shows Colucci's view of how AI and related technology is changing the legal profession.

Colucci says that data and data analysis support the higher-value levels in this "AI in Law" pyramid. Data can be used to support vertical expertise, which can help a defendant, plaintiff, or lawyer to be more effective. Examples are analyzing past cases to determine the best strategy for a case, such as the most favorable jurisdiction, attorney, court, or judge.

Complex legal reasoning, says Colucci, will always be the purview of humans, with their detailed knowledge of the world that is unlikely to be replicated by computers anytime in the near future. "Good lawyering," says Colucci, "will always be the secret sauce separating us from the machines."

So how can technology help? DI combines models based on historical information as captured in data and analyzed by AI with models of the world provided by humans.

Figure 70. How DI Enhances Legal Reasoning.

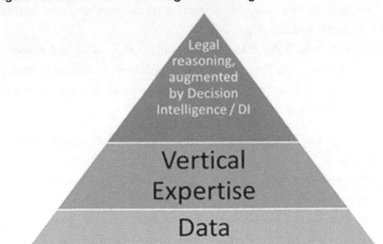

KNOWLEDGE GARDENS

Jack Park's Topic Quests Knowledge Gardens initiative [196] is driving innovations in visual and interactive representations of online collaboration to support "wicked conversations".

Park says that part of the reason for the effectiveness of game-based conversations is that because people work through avatars, the ego is suppressed, leading to more effective problem-solving. Says Park, "When a human is controlling an avatar, some very important psychological benefits are in play ... they are less likely to inject their personal identities, their personalities, and their biases into the game." This facilitates "[...] the transition from me to we [...] the entire process shifts from egocentric to ecocentric." Park's work also involves creating visual representations of knowledge structures.

GANDHISM, TRUSTEESHIP, AND COMBATING WEALTH INEQUALITY THROUGH DI

Gandhi predicted that both capitalism and communism would eventually fail [197]. He proposed a third system, called *trusteeship* [198] which held tremendous promise. Yet today's world is much more complex than the one that Gandhi inhabited, and so we need new technologies to navigate the maze of the complex adaptive system that characterizes our cultural, economic, and political reality.

Ferose and Pratt [199] describes a vision for this social and economic shift, and includes a description of how DI can help this initiative to manage the complexities of incorporating checks and balances into such a system. The article argues that

> *Data, AI, and DI are powerful weapons against such exploitation because they allow us to, respectively, 1) obtain direct and voluminous empirical evidence regarding human behavior; 2) analyze the data to understand and predict the outcomes of certain events; and 3) choose actions to initiate chains of events that simultaneously achieve desirable individual, organizational, and societal outcomes.*

A related new initiative by Kamesh Raghavendra and VR Ferose is developing a wealth equity index (WEI) to address widespread global wealth inequality using market forces. Similar to "green" measures of companies, this index uses market forces to grow companies whose activities decrease wealth inequality worldwide. This happens through a multi-step chain of events. For this reason, the success of this initiative depends on an understanding of multi-link economic flows. These must be understood not just by economists but by the population at large.

One potential mechanism is shown in Figure 71. It shows how sovereign wealth funds (like Alaska's initiative that sends a check to all state residents every year) invests in a VC fund, which in turn invests in companies. Those companies receive a "red," "green," or "yellow" WEI label, indicating the degree to which their success benefits the bottom 80%.

Consumers looking to reduce wealth inequality then will preferentially choose to buy products from "yellow" or "green" WEI firms, thus driving value for all members of value chain, and ultimately benefiting the lower 80% of the wealth holders in the economy.

As of this writing, the WEI initiative has not yet been announced, and the particulars of the model may change, but the need for a good understanding of how multi-link effects play out over time is essential to its success.

Figure 71. One Mechanism by Which the Wealth Equality Index Can Redistribute Wealth to the Bottom 80%.

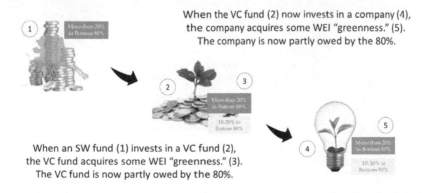

When the VC fund (2) now invests in a company (4), the company acquires some WEI "greenness." (5). The company is now partly owed by the 80%.

When an SW fund (1) invests in a VC fund (2), the VC fund acquires some WEI "greenness." (3). The VC fund is now partly owed by the 80%.

Ferose, who heads SAP's Engineering Academy, says:

Drastic changes are needed to reverse trends towards inequality worldwide, and the WEI index is one mechanism that can make a big difference. To successfully, transparently, and collaboratively model and manage the effectiveness of any initiative this complex will depend on both good AI/data science models, as well as presentation within a cause-and-effect model flow. Trust in these models will be essential, so we need methods that are both understandable and sophisticated, which is true for DI models. [200]

CONCLUSION

We are both socially and technologically on the precipice of evolving into a future-thinking species — a transformation that we desperately need. In order to hasten this shift, we must ensure that individuals and communities are not being left behind while only a small population benefits from social and technological advancements.

People are afraid of massive changes [...] and many are attempting to hold onto a world that has become obsolete. To avoid a global backlash that will lead to some very undesirable outcomes for humanity, we must democratize the future and make the benefits of this transformation available to everyone.

— Frank Spencer/Yvette Montero Salvatico
(*Kedge/The Futures School* [1])

Decision intelligence (DI) is the most important initiative of the twenty-first century. Although the field is young, it represents a promising, practical, and focused approach to taming the complexities we face in many arenas. Whether you come at the field as a technologist like me, or whether your approach begins with economics, anthropology, management science, or you're a student or retiree, you'll find in DI a convergence for an exciting solutions renaissance. Indeed,

> **Key Insight #58:** Given the interdependent nature of wicked problems, one view is that they are all facets of the *same* problem: the emergence of new dynamics in an interconnected global world — especially winner-takes-all feedback effects — which we must understand and manage.

This is only the beginning, and along the way we'll experience transient oscillations. Characteristic of any major phase shift, this turbulence should not be confused with the end state, which will represent a rewiring of how humans interact with their social, technical, and natural worlds [201].

The progress to date is slow but steady. As you have read here, there are many DI initiatives. And they are growing: each one of the items in the "DI as" items in Chapter 5, could, for example, be embraced by an academic or a new company. Or, even if you are a student or individual, you could begin a DI salon or meetup to discuss important current events — along with the assumptions, facts, and more underlying them — and by making them explicit, to contribute to collaborative solutions that go beyond conversations.

In short, DI is about turning wicked problems into "Wicked Opportunities" [202]. And you, by finishing this book, have joined the DI "Tribe." I welcome you, and invite you to continue on this journey with us.

Peace,
Lorien Pratt
Santa Cruz, California, March 2019.

ACKNOWLEDGMENTS

Decision intelligence (DI) as a field is ambitious and collaborative, and this book reflects this pattern in microcosm. Although my name may be on the cover page, this work represents contributions from thousands of people worldwide who are joining this important movement. I'll name a few of those who have helped here below, but my first statement is of gratitude to this larger set of contributors.

Of particular note: the ideas and words in this book derived in large part from thousands of conversations with Mark Zangari over a 15-year period. Mark and I co-founded Quantellia in 2010; much of this book derives from my experiences there. Also, the our team's hard work and investor's funding has given me the bandwidth to complete it. Their generosity of spirit, vision, and trust in me is above and beyond. I am particularly grateful to our COO Nadine Malcolm, who took on much of the day-to-day company operations as I became less available during the final weeks of writing.

Over the years, a number of DI visionaries and companies have emerged who together helped to move the DI ecosystem forward. It takes a special kind of person to see the future, even moreso to help to design it. Jim Casart, Sammy Thomas, Jennifer Fruehauf, Göran Källmark, Håkan Edvinsson, Avi Hauser, and the teams at Avaya Government Solutions (especially Arlow Julian and Linda Kemp), Informed Decisions, Cisco, and Cognizant were particularly supportive in our early days. More recently, we're very grateful to Nick Stavrou at QRisk Strategies; Ian Oliver and Jennifer Horwood at Versant Solutions; and VR Ferose at SAP.[1] Early visionaries Janet Nemmers, Allie Golon, and Liesl Inouye also deserve our utmost gratitude.

A few who deserve special mention: Linda Kemp, who worked diligently to bring DI into the US government; Rick Ladd, whose "Systems Savvy" blog helped to validate DI to the world; Steve Brant, who wrote in Medium about decision intelligence; Karl Whitelock, who wrote the first industry analyst report on DI; and Rob Rich, who wrote the second. Valerie Landau is also a DI visionary whose work with Doug Englebart and others has a deep relationship to the work described here. Margaret Johnson created the Decision Intelligence Institute International (TDI3) ecosystem. More recently, I've also had the pleasure of meeting Cassie Kozyrkov, whose DI work at Google Cloud has helped to solidify and shape the definition of DI; and the work of Frank Spencer and Yvette Montero Salvatico, at Kedge/The Futures School, who I met in the last day of writing, overlaps substantially with the vision here, and who have been evangelizing it worldwide within Disney, nonprofits, commercial companies, and governments.

I would also like to thank the team that rolled up their sleeves to get the book contracted and completed. My agent Jeanne Levine brought her years of relationships within the publishing industry to help me to navigate through a flurry of proposals to the perfect publisher for this work, Emerald Publishing, where Charlotte Maiorana has been an enthusiastic and visionary supporter of the book. Emily Zhao, Rick Ladd, Jessica Jaret, and Elizabeth Nitz helped with social media, and Rick Ladd, Elizabeth Nitz, and Nadine Malcolm helped with figures and bibliography, and also thoroughly copy-edited an early draft. Nadine was, in particular, the driving force behind the design of many of the figures in this book.

External reviewers included Richard Smith, Faith Hopp, Guy Pfeffermann, Beza Getahun, Annis Pratt, Jim Casart, Håkan Edvinsson, Bill Fenwick, Ruth Fisher, Valerie Landau, and Jack Park. Their insights provided a "final polish" to the book, improving its quality noticeably.

Thanks as well to my family: Annis Pratt, Deb Vilas, and Faith Hopp, who supported me during this audacious endeavor, and Cymbre and Griffin Smith, the world's first "native" decision modelers.

NOTE

1. www.responsibleaidi.org

BIBLIOGRAPHY

[1] F. Spencer, *Personal Communication*, February 2019.

[2] V. Ferose, L. Pratt, S. Dasgupta and G. Subramanian, "The Birth of the Inclusion Ecosystem: Precision Employment for People with Disabilities, Coolabilities, and the Rest of Us," in V. Cerf & D. Nordfors (Eds.), *The People Centered Economy: The New Ecosystem For Work*, Palo Alto, CA: IIIJ Foundation, 2018, p. 394. [Online]. Available: https://www.amazon.com/People-Centered-Economy-Ecosystem-Work/dp/1729145922/ref=tmm_pap_swatch_0?_encoding=UTF8&qid=&sr=. [Accessed 7 February 2019].

[3] L. Pratt, "The Magical Diminishing Returns Link, and Why It Can Fix Government Budgeting (and Yours, Too)," 6 March 2015. [Online]. Available: https://www.lorienpratt.com/the-magical-diminishing-returns-link-and-why-it-can-fix-government-budgeting-and-yours-too/. [Accessed 9 March 2019].

[4] B. Marr, "The Amazing Ways How Mastercard Uses Artificial Intelligence To Stop Fraud and Reduce False Declines," 30 November 2018. [Online]. Available: https://www.forbes.com/sites/bernardmarr/2018/11/30/the-amazing-ways-how-mastercard-uses-artificial-intelligence-to-stop-fraud-and-reduce-false-declines/#280b3e542165. [Accessed 11 February 2019].

[5] Alibaba, "Decision Intelligence Lab." [Online]. Available: https://damo.alibaba.com/labs/decision-intelligence. [Accessed 11 February 2019].

[6] J. Parr, *Personal Communication*, February 2019.

[7] C. Byrne, "Why Google Defined a New Discipline to Help Humans Make Decisions," Fast Company, 18 July 2018. [Online]. Available:

https://www.fastcompany.com/90203073/why-google-defined-a-new-discipline-to-help-humans-make-decisions. [Accessed 23 January 2019]

[8] V. R. Ferose and L. Pratt, "How AI Is Disrupting the Law," *Digitalist Magazine*, 3 April 2018. Available: https://www.digitalistmag.com/digital-economy/2018/04/03/ai-is-disrupting-law-06030693

[9] M. Nickelsburg, "Element Data Raises $3.5M to Help Companies Make Decisions with A.I. and Machine Learning," GeekWire, 12 July 2017. [Online]. Available: https://www.geekwire.com/2017/element-data-raises-3-5m-powered-decision-making-engine/. [Accessed 28 January 2019].

[10] Tech Expert, "Prowler.io Nabs $13M for Its New Approach to Decision Making in AI," Technews, 4 September 2017. [Online]. Available: http://technewsexpert.com/prowler-io-nabs-13m-for-its-new-approach-to-decision-making-in-ai/. [Accessed 28 January 2019].

[11] J. Kerbel, "Thinking Straight: Cognitive Bias in the US Debate about China," Central Intelligence Agency Library, 14 April 2007. [Online]. Available: https://www.cia.gov/library/center-for-the-study-of-intelligence/csi-publications/csi-studies/studies/vol48no3/article03.html. [Accessed 24 January 2014].

[12] D. Pontefract, "Don't Be Afraid to Call Yourself a Neo-generalist," 3 January 2019. [Online]. Available: https://www.forbes.com/sites/workday/2019/01/03/how-were-helping-you-prepare-for-ifrs-17/#264be74566fd. [Accessed 11 January 2018].

[13] T. S. Kuhn, *The Copernican Revolution*, Cambridge, MA: Harvard University Press, 1985.

[14] H. Bloom, *Global Brain: The Evolution of Mass Mind from the Big Bang to the 21st Century*, New York, NY: John Wiley & Sons, 2000.

[15] C. Kozyrkov, *Personal Communication*, February 2019.

[16] E. Clegg, "Master Symbols: A Visual Insight Field Guide: Book One," Bodega Bay, CA: Visual Insight Press, 2018. [Online]. Available: https://www.visualinsight.net/product/master-symbols/

[17] G. Lakoff, "Understanding Trump," The University of Chicago Press books, August 2016. [Online]. Available: https://georgelakoff.com/2016/07/23/understanding-trump-2/. [Accessed 5 January 2019].

[18] M. Fay, "Foreign Policy and Defense," Niskanen Center, 1 August 2016. [Online]. Available: https://niskanencenter.org/blog/defense-reform-unintended-consequences/. [Accessed 29 January 2019].

[19] J. Casart, *Personal Communication,* 2019.

[20] M. Hobbes, "Stop Trying to Save the World," The New Republic, 17 November 2014. [Online]. Available: https://newrepublic.com/article/120178/problem-international-development-and-plan-fix-it. [Accessed 29 January 2019].

[21] R. L. Martin, "Rethinking the Decision Factory," Harvard Business Review, October 2013. [Online]. Available: https://hbr.org/2013/10/rethinking-the-decision-factory. [Accessed 11 January 2019].

[22] L. Pratt and M. Zangari, "High Performance Decision Making: A Global Study," 7 January 2009. [Online]. Available: https://quantellia.com/Data/HighPerformanceDecisionMaking.pdf. [Accessed 28 January 2019].

[23] Judea Pearl, *The Book of Why: The New Science of Cause and Effect,* London: Basic Books, 2018, p. 432. [Online]. Available: https://www.amazon.com/Book-Why-Science-Cause-Effect/dp/046509760X. [Accessed 11 January 2019].

[24] A. Watts, *The Wisdom of Insecurity,* New York, NY: Random House Inc., 1979.

[25] Object Management Group®, "Unified Modeling Language," Object Management Group, 2019. [Online]. Available: http://www.uml.org/. [Accessed 29 January 2019].

[26] D. Kahneman, "Thinking, Fast and Slow," Farrar, Straus and Giroux, 2011. [Online]. Available: https://www.amazon.com/Thinking-Fast-Slow-Daniel-Kahneman/dp/0374533555

[27] Quantellia LLC, "Data from the Future," [Online]. Available: https://youtu.be/UqkZOGoN_Wo. [Accessed 11 February 2019].

[28] Several, "Transfer Learning," Wikipedia, [Online]. Available: https://
      en.wikipedia.org/wiki/Transfer_learning. [Accessed 07 February 2019].

[29] S. Thrun and L. Pratt, *Learning to Learn*, Norwell, MA: Kluwer
      Academic Publishers, 1998.

[30] L. Y. Pratt, L. L. Tracy and M. Noordewier, "Back-propagation
      Learning on Ribosomal Binding Sites in DNA Sequences Using
      Preprocessed Features," in *Proceedings of the IEEE International
      Conference on Neural Networks, IEEE World Congress on
      Computational Intelligence*, Vol. 5, pp. 3332–3335, 1994, IEEE.
      Available: https://pdfs.semanticscholar.org/7572/
      10804947d0a78628b2a7ea14b902248fb9f5.pdf

[31] Quantellia, "Quantellia Helps US Federal Courts Reduce IT
      Infrastructure Budget By 15%," 2013, Quantellia.com. [Online].
      Available: https://quantellia.com/quantellia-helps-us-federal-courts-
      reduce-it-infrastructure/. [Accessed 07 February 2019].

[32] W. Kenton, "Winner-Takes-All Market," Investopedia, 29 January
      2018. [Online]. Available: https://www.investopedia.com/terms/w/
      winner-takes-all-market.asp. [Accessed 11 January 2019].

[33] R. Fisher, *Personal Communication,* 2019.

[34] H. Haq, "Starbucks Raises Prices – Again. Why Customers Will Still
      Drink Up," The Christian Science Monitor, 7 July 2016. [Online].
      Available: https://www.csmonitor.com/Business/The-Bite/2015/0707/
      Starbucks-raises-prices-again.-Why-customers-will-still-drink-up.
      [Accessed 11 January 2019].

[35] C. G. Jung, *The Archetypes and the Collective Unconscious*,
      Princeton, NJ: Princeton University Press, 1981. [Online]. Available:
      https://books.google.com/books?id=Yc5PlU9MyDwC

[36] L. Pratt, "Getting Ahead of the Curve: Understanding Cable Energy
      Decisions," YouTube, 19 August 2015. [Online]. Available: https://
      www.youtube.com/watch?v=hUiVk-ld3OE&t=79s. [Accessed
      11 January 2019].

[37] L. Pratt and M. Zangari, "The System Dynamics of Aid,
      Understanding the Carter Center's CJA Program in Liberia,"

Quantellia, 25 January 2014. [Online]. Available: https://quantellia.
com/Data/System-dynamics-of-aid-Pratt-Zangari-2014.pdf. [Accessed
11 January 2019].

[38] Quantellia, "Frontline Health Workers at Tiyatien Health: Reducing
Child Mortality," Youtube, 25 January 2014. [Online]. Available:
https://www.youtube.com/watch?v=gdyTN674WwQ. [Accessed 11
January 2019].

[39] L. Pratt, "Announcing Interactive Web-based Decision Intelligence,"
25 April 2015. [Online]. Available: https://www.lorienpratt.com/
announcing-interactive-web-based-decision-intelligence/. [Accessed
29 January 2019].

[40] Quantellia, "Wow! How to Use Big Data and Machine Learning to
Solve 1,000s of New Problems," YouTube, 9 November 2014.
[Online]. Available: https://youtu.be/5kXTHe4vX3k. [Accessed
29 January 2019].

[41] Google, Inc., "Google Ngram Viewer for Unintended Consequences,"
[Online]. Available: https://books.google.com/ngrams/graph?content=
%22unintended+consequences%22&year_start=1940&year_end=
2000&corpus=15&smoothing=3&share=&direct_url=t1%3B%2C%
22%20unintended%20consequences%20%22%3B%2Cc0. [Accessed
5 April 2019].

[42] L. Pratt and M. Zangari, "The New Science of Decision Engineering,"
Telecom Asia, 8 September 2008, pp. 20–22. [Online]. Available:
https://www.telecomasia.net/content/new-science-decision-engineering-
0. [Accessed 28 January 2019].

[43] H. Edvinsson, *Personal Communication*, 2019.

[44] C. Grundwag, "Coolabilities — A New Language for Strengths in
Disabling Conditions," in D. Nordfors & V. Cerf (Eds.), *The People
Centered Economy: The New Ecosystem for Work*, Palo Alto, CA: IIIJ
Foundation, 2018, pp. 173–185.

[45] C. Kozyrkov, "Decision Intelligence (ML++)," Tech Open Air,
9 August 2018. [Online]. Available: https://www.youtube.com/watch?
v=Qr4P_jCdUFs. [Accessed 29 January 2019].

[46] Quantellia LLC, "Carbon Tax Demonstration Decision Model," quantellia.com, 2014. [Online]. Available: https://quantellia.com/ OMEGAModel/omega-h.html. [Accessed 29 January 2019].

[47] I. Asimov, *Asimov on Science Fiction*, Garden City, NY: Doubleday, 1981.

[48] J. McMullen, *Personal Communication*, 2019.

[49] G. Bateson, *Mind and Nature: A Necessary Unity*, New York, NY: Dutton, 1979. [Online]. Available: http://famousquotefrom.com/ gregory-bateson/. [Accessed 2 February 2019].

[50] Wikipedia, "Wicked Problem," 14 December 2018. [Online]. Available: https://en.wikipedia.org/wiki/Wicked_problem. [Accessed 11 January 2018].

[51] J. C. Glenn, E. Florescu and T. M. P. Team, "State of the Future Version 19.1, 19.1 ed.," 2015. [Online]. Available: http://www. millennium-project.org/state-of-the-future-version-19-1/. [Accessed 5 April 2019].

[52] The Millennium Project, "Challenge 5. How Can Decisionmaking Be Enhanced by Integrating Improved Global Foresight during Unprecedented Accelerating Change?," The Millennium Project, 2017. [Online]. Available: http://www.millennium-project.org/challenge-5/. [Accessed 11 January 2019].

[53] M. Jones and P. Silberzahn, "Snowden and the Challenge of Intelligence: The Practical Case Against the NSA's Big Data," *Forbes*, 11 July 2013. [Online]. Available: https://www.forbes.com/sites/ silberzahnjones/2013/07/11/snowden-and-the-challenge-of-intelligence-the-practical-case-against-nsa-big-data/#3855014d5f4b. [Accessed 4 February 2019].

[54] S. Stephens-Davidowitz and H. Varian, "A Hands-on Guide to Google Data," 7 March 2015. [Online]. Available: http://sethsd.com/research/. [Accessed 3 February 2019].

[55] A. Chang, "What Can Google Search Data Tell Us about Human Behavior?," All Things Considered, *NPR*, 6 August 2018. Seth Stephens-Davidowitz interview. [Online]. Available: https://www.npr.

org/2018/08/06/636112882/what-can-google-search-data-tell-us-about-human-behavior. [Accessed 3 February 2019].

[56] D. Kosecki, "How Much Sleep Do Fitbit Users Really Get? A New Study Finds Out," Fitbit, 29 June 2017. [Online]. Available: https://blog.fitbit.com/sleep-study/. [Accessed 3 February 2019].

[57] D. Kosecki, "A New Champion Has Been Crowned: Check Out 2017's Fittest Cities!," Fitbit News, 15 May 2017. [Online]. Available: https://blog.fitbit.com/fittest-cities-in-america/. [Accessed 3 February 2019].

[58] USAID, "Spatial Data Repository." [Online]. Available: http://spatialdata.dhsprogram.com/home/. [Accessed 3 February 2019].

[59] A. Freedman, "U.S. Readies Big-Data Dump on Climate and Weather," Mashable, 24 February 2014. [Online]. Available: https://mashable.com/2014/02/24/noaa-data-cloud/#osT0KR.4jiqw. [Accessed 11 January 2019].

[60] F. Banfi, E. Hazan and A. Levy, *Using "Big Data" to Optimize Digital Marketing*, New York, McKinsey Insights, McKinsey & Company, April 2013. [Online]. Available: https://www.mckinsey.com/business-functions/marketing-and-sales/our-insights/using-big-data-to-optimize-digital-marketing. [Accessed 3 February 2019].

[61] B. Kayyali, D. Knott and S. Van Kuiken, *How Big Data Is Shaping US Health Care*, New York, McKinsey Quarterly, McKinsey & Company, May 2013. [Online]. Available: https://www.mckinsey.com/industries/healthcare-systems-and-services/our-insights/how-big-data-is-shaping-us-health-care. [Accessed 3 February 2019].

[62] RECAP Project, "RECAP Project — Turning PACER around since 2009," 2018. [Online]. Available: https://free.law/recap/. [Accessed 3 February 2019].

[63] News Room, "Companies Struggling to Operationalize Big Data," TM Forum, May 2016. [Online]. Available: http://inform.tmforum.org/news/2016/05/companies-struggling-to-operationalize-big-data/. [Accessed 11 January 2019].

[64] D. Henschen, "Microsoft's Big Data Strategy: An Insider's View," Information Week, 23 February 2013. [Online]. Available: http://www.

informationweek.com/big-data/big-data-analytics/microsofts-big-data-strategy-an-insiders-view/d/d-id/1108641. [Accessed 11 January 2019].

[65] N. Bateson, *Personal Communication*, 4 March 2019.

[66] Zoolingua, "Zoolingua," 2019. [Online]. Available: www.zoolingua.com. [Accessed 11 January 2019].

[67] L. Feng, "The Future of AI: Funding Accelerates for AI Startups," Forbes, 30 January 2018. [Online]. Available: https://www.forbes.com/sites/forbescommunicationscouncil/2018/01/30/the-future-of-ai-funding-accelerates-for-ai-startups/#c72e99658ab4. [Accessed 11 January 2019].

[68] V. Barhat, "China Is Determined to Steal A.I. Crown from US and Nothing, Not Even a Trade War, Will Stop It," CNBC, 4 May 2018. [Online]. Available: https://www.cnbc.com/2018/05/04/china-aims-to-steal-us-a-i-crown-and-not-even-trade-war-will-stop-it.html. [Accessed 11 January 2019].

[69] S. Lohr, "Microsoft, Amid Dwindling Interest, Talks Up Computing as a Career," New York Times, 1 March 2004. [Online]. Available: https://www.nytimes.com/2004/03/01/business/microsoft-amid-dwindling-interest-talks-up-computing-as-a-career.html. [Accessed 3 February 2019].

[70] D. Galeon, "Obama: Synthetic Intelligence Will Totally Transform Our Future," 13 October 2016. [Online]. Futurism. Available: https://futurism.com/president-obama-weighs-in-on-how-synthetic-intelligence-is-transforming-our-future/. [Accessed 3 February 2019].

[71] L. Pratt, "Machine Learning Is Poised for Mass Adoption," Quantellia, 12 October 2015. [Online]. Available: https://www.lorienpratt.com/machine-learning-is-poised-for-mass-adoption/. [Accessed 11 January 2019].

[72] L. Pratt, L. L. Tracy and M. Noordewier, "Back-propagation Learning on Ribosomal Binding Sites in DNA Sequences Using Preprocessed Features," in *Proceedings of the IEEE International Conference on Neural Networks, IEEE World Congress on Computational Intelligence*, Vol. 5, pp. 3332–3335, 1994, IEEE. Available: https://

ieeexplore.ieee.org/xpl/tocresult.jsp?isnumber=8558&filter%3DAND
(p_IS_Number:8558)%26pageNumber%3D5=&pageNumber=1

[73] M. Misra, L. Y. Pratt, C. Farris and R. O. Hansen, "Neural Network
Analysis for Hazardous Waste Characterization," in P. E. Keller, S.
Hashem, L. J. Kangas & R. T. Kouzes (Eds.), *Applications of Neural
Networks in Environment, Energy, and Health*, World Scientific
Publishing Co.: Singapore, 1996.

[74] M. S. Verma, L. Pratt, C. Ganesh and C. Medina, "Hair-MAP: A
prototype Automated System for Forensic Hair Comparison and
Analysis," *Forensic Science International, vol. 129*, no. 3,
pp. 168–186, 2002.

[75] Wikipedia, "Fifth Generation Computer," Wikipedia, 20 January
2019. [Online]. Available: https://en.wikipedia.org/wiki/Fifth_
generation_computer. [Accessed 4 February 2019].

[76] Wikipedia, "Cyc," 24 January 2019. [Online]. Available: https://en.
wikipedia.org/wiki/Cyc. [Accessed 4 February 2019].

[77] M. Frontain, "Microelectronics and Computer Technology
Corporation [MCC]," Texas State Historical Association, Handbook
of Texas Online, 15 June 2010. [Online]. Available: https://tshaonline.
org/handbook/online/articles/dnm01. [Accessed 4 February 2019].

[78] Wikipedia, "Alvey," 21 September 2018. [Online]. Available: https://
en.wikipedia.org/wiki/Alvey. [Accessed 4 February 2019].

[79] Prowler.io, "Using VUKU for Logistics," [Online]. Available: https://
www.prowler.io/platform/logistics. [Accessed 09 February 2019].

[80] Wikipedia, "Decision Tree Learning," 10 January 2019. [Online].
Available: https://en.wikipedia.org/wiki/Decision_tree_learning.
[Accessed 11 January 2019].

[81] Wikipedia, "Decision Tree," 10 January 2019. [Online]. Available:
https://en.wikipedia.org/wiki/Decision_tree_learning. [Accessed
11 January 2019].

[82] T. Stephens, "UCSC Team Wins Cancer Genomics Competition," UC
Santa Cruz, 8 October 2013. [Online]. Available: https://news.ucsc.edu/
2013/11/dream-competition.html. [Accessed 11 January 2019].

[83] "Artificial Intelligence: How We Help Machines Learn," The New York Times, 2019. [Online]. The New York Times. Available: https://www.nytimes.com/paidpost/facebook/artificial-intelligence-how-we-help-machines-learn.html. [Accessed 11 January 2019].

[84] N. Wiener, *Cybernetics: Or Control and Communication in the Animal and the Machine*, Cambridge, MA: MIT Press, 1948. [Online]. Available: https://en.wikipedia.org/wiki/Cybernetics:_Or_Control_and_Communication_in_the_Animal_and_the_Machine#cite_note-1

[85] Wikipedia, "Human–Computer Interaction," 24 January 2019. [Online]. Available: https://en.wikipedia.org/wiki/Human%E2%80%93computer_interaction. [Accessed 4 February 2019].

[86] W. S. McCulloch and W. Pitts, "A Logical Calculus of the Ideas Immanent in Nervous Activity," *The Bulletin of Mathematical Biophysics*, vol. 5, no. 4, pp. 115–133, December 1943. [Online]. Available: https://link.springer.com/article/10.1007/BF02478259

[87] The Cybernetics Society, "The Cybernetics Society," 11 November 2018. [Online]. Available: http://www.cybsoc.org/. [Accessed 4 February 2019].

[88] Google Trends, "Google Trends," 4 February 2019. [Online]. Available: https://trends.google.com/trends/explore?date=all&geo=US&q=artificial%20intelligence,cybernetics. [Accessed 4 February 2019].

[89] P. M. Asaro, "Cybernetics," 2010. [Online]. Available: http://www.peterasaro.org/writing/Cybernetics.html. [Accessed 4 February 2019].

[90] D. J. Snowden and M. E. Boone, "A Leader's Framework for Decision Making," *Harvard Business Review*, 85(11):68–76, 149, 2007. [Online]. Available: https://hbr.org/2007/11/a-leaders-framework-for-decision-making

[91] M. Mitchell, *Complexity: A Guided Tour*, New York, NY: Oxford University Press, 2011. [Online]. Available: https://www.amazon.com/Complexity-Guided-Tour-Melanie-Mitchell/dp/0199798109

[92] J. Casart, *Personal Communication*, 2018.

[93] S. Ronis, *Personal Communication*, 2019.

[94] Kedge Futures, "Kedge Futures," 2018. [Online]. Available: https://kedgefutures.com/. [Accessed 5 February 2019].

[95] The OR Society, "Learn About O.R.," 2012. [Online]. Available: http://www.learnaboutor.co.uk/. [Accessed 11 January 2019].

[96] The OR Society, "Introduction to Operational Research," YouTube, 9 November 2012. [Online]. Available: https://www.youtube.com/watch?v=QzSWMw4P8x8. [Accessed 11 January 2019].

[97] World Makers, "World Makers," 2019. [Online]. Available: http://simulate.world/summary/. [Accessed 11 January 2019].

[98] A. Hook, *Personal Communication*, 2019.

[99] L. Pratt, "The World Resources Sim Center: On Its Way to Silicon Valley," Quantellia, 4 January 2016. [Online]. Available: http://www.lorienpratt.com/the-world-resources-sim-center-on-its-way-to-silicon-valley/. [Accessed 11 January 2019].

[100] L. Pratt, "Models," [Online]. Available: https://www.lorienpratt.com/how-can-i-help-you/resources/models/. [Accessed 5 February 2019].

[101] R. O'Neil, *Personal Communication*, 2019.

[102] G. S. McChrystal and C. Fussell, "Team of Teams: New Rules of Engagement for a Complex World, Portfolio Hardcover," New York, NY, 2015. Available: https://www.amazon.com/Team-Teams-Rules-Engagement-Complex/dp/1591847486

[103] Wikipedia, "Whac-A-Mole," 4 November 2018. [Online]. Available: https://en.wikipedia.org/wiki/Whac-A-Mole. [Accessed 11 January 2019].

[104] R. B. Fuller, *Synergetics: Explorations in the Geometry of Thinking*, New York, NY: Macmillan Publishing Company, 1982. [Online]. Available: https://www.amazon.com/Synergetics-Explorations-Geometry-Buckminster-Fuller/dp/0020653204

[105] J. Brewer, "What If It's All Connected? Humanity and the Global Crisis," 22 March 2016. [Online]. Available: https://www.kosmosjournal.org/news/what-if-its-all-connected-humanity-and-the-global-crisis/. [Accessed 11 January 2019].

[106] J. W. Forrester, "Forrester Seminar Series," System Dynamics, 2018. [Online]. Available: https://www.systemdynamics.org/forrester-seminar-series. [Accessed 11 January 2019].

[107] Google, Inc., "Google Trends," [Online]. Available: https://trends.google.com/trends/explore?date=all&geo=US&q=%22big%20data%22,%22artificial%20intelligence%22,%22machine%20learning%22,%22system%20dynamics%22,%22complex%20systems%22. [Accessed 5 April 2019].

[108] Wikipedia, "Escalation Archetype," 20 September 2017. [Online]. Available: https://en.wikipedia.org/wiki/Escalation_archetype. [Accessed 11 January 2019].

[109] S. Brant, "Russell Ackoff, 'Einstein of Problem Solving,' Has Died," HuffPost, 6 December 2017. [Online]. Available: https://www.huffingtonpost.com/steven-g-brant/russell-ackoff—the-eins_b_341349.html. [Accessed 11 January 2019].

[110] N. Bateson, "An Ecology of Mind – A Daughter's Portrait of Gregory Bateson Directed by Nora Bateson," Vimeo, 13 January 2015. [Online]. Available: https://vimeo.com/ondemand/bateson/116642860. [Accessed 11 January 2019].

[111] B. Kort, "The Ninth Intelligence," Gallimaufrey, 6 September 2013. [Online]. Available: https://barrykort.wordpress.com/2013/09/06/the-ninth-intelligence/. [Accessed 11 January 2019].

[112] Sustainable Human, "How Wolves Change Rivers," YouTube, 13 February 2014. [Online]. Available: https://www.youtube.com/watch?v=ysa5OBhXz-Q. [Accessed 11 January 2019].

[113] A. Tabarrok, "Harry Potter and the Mystery of Inequality," 23 August 2007. [Online]. Available: https://marginalrevolution.com/marginalrevolution/2007/04/harry_potter_an.html. [Accessed 31 January 2019].

[114] S. Rosen, "The Economics of Superstars," *The American Economic Review*, *vol. 71*, pp. 845–858, American Economic Association, December 1981. [Online]. Available: http://www.uvm.edu/pdodds/files/papers/others/1981/rosen1981a.pdf. [Accessed 1 March 2019].

[115] D. S. Evans, A. Hagiu and R. Schmalensee, *Invisible Engines: How Software Platforms Drive Innovation and Transform Industries*, 1 ed., Cambridge, MA: The MIT Press, 2008, p. 409. [Online]. Available: https://www.amazon.com/dp/B002R0DR8I/ref=dp-kindle-redirect?_encoding=UTF8&btkr=1

[116] C. C. Gilbert Le Bouar, "An Analysis of the Risk in the French Sea Fishing Industry. Example of the Dockside Accident Risk," International Maritime Health, Medical University of Gdańsk, 2006. [Online]. Available: https://imh.mug.edu.pl/attachment/attachment/5258/R11.pdf. [Accessed 11 January 2019].

[117] Responsible AIDI Summit, "AI/DI in Action – RAIDI Summit 2018," 4 December 2018. [Online]. Available: www.responsibleaidi.org. [Accessed 5 February 2019].

[118] M. C. Jackson, *Systems Approaches to Management*, Springer, 2000. [Online]. Available: https://www.amazon.com/Systems-Approaches-Management-Michael-Jackson/dp/0306465000

[119] M. Zangari, Teaching Computers to Think Like Decision Makers. [Performance]. 24 May 2014. [Online]. Available https://www.youtube.com/watch?v=CfQznGK98bI.

[120] A. Linn, "Microsoft Researchers Win ImageNet Computer Vision Challenge," 10 December 2015. [Online]. Available: https://blogs.microsoft.com/ai/microsoft-researchers-win-imagenet-computer-vision-challenge/. [Accessed 11 January 2019].

[121] Wikipedia, "Transfer Learning," 31 December 2018. [Online]. Available: https://en.wikipedia.org/wiki/Transfer_learning. [Accessed 11 January 2019].

[122] L. Pratt, Ed. "Special Issue: Reuse of Neural Networks through Transfer," *Connection Science, vol. 8*, no. 2, 1996.

[123] L. Pratt and S. Thrun, Eds. "Second Special Issue on Inductive Transfer," in *Machine Learning*, Kluwer Academic Press, 1997.

[124] C. Davis, *Personal Communication*, 2019.

[125] B. Pell, "Crucial Questions for Applying AI," Creative Destruction
Lab, 9 November 2016. [Online]. Available: https://www.youtube.
com/watch?v=IvFcilMKvfQ. [Accessed 5 March 2019].

[126] D. Woods, "The Man-Machine Framework: How to Build Machine-
Learning Applications the Right Way," 18 October 2012. [Online].
Available: https://www.forbes.com/sites/danwoods/2012/10/18/the-
man-machine-framework-how-to-build-machine-learning-applications-
the-right-way/#5c866c6c7e20. [Accessed 11 January 2019].

[127] N. N. Taleb, "The Black Swan: Second Edition: The Impact of the
Highly Improbable," New York, NY: Random House Trade
Paperbacks, 11 May 2010. [Online]. Available: https://www.amazon.
com/Black-Swan-Improbable-Robustness-Fragility/dp/081297381X

[128] V. Landau, E. Clegg and D. Englebart, *The Engelbart Hypothesis:
Dialogs with Douglas Engelbart*, 2 ed., NextPresss, 2009. [Online].
Available: https://www.amazon.com/dp/B003MAK5E6/ref=dp-kindle-
redirect?_encoding=UTF8&btkr=1

[129] V. Landau, *Personal Communication*, 2019.

[130] Stanford, "Decision Analysis Graduate Certificate," 2018. [Online].
Available: https://scpd.stanford.edu/public/category/
courseCategoryCertificateProfile.do?method=load&certificateId=
73464315. [Accessed 11 January 2019].

[131] Society of Decision Professionals, 2019. [Online]. Available:
https://www.decisionprofessionals.com/. [Accessed 11 January 2019].

[132] D. Charlesworth, *Decision Analysis for Managers: A Guide for
Making Better Personal and Business Decisions*, 2 ed. Massachusetts,
MA: Business Expert Press, 2017. Available: https://www.
businessexpertpress.com/

[133] Decision Analysis Society, 2019. [Online]. Available: https://connect.
informs.org/das/home. [Accessed 28 January 2019].

[134] TransparentChoice, "Transparent Choice," 2018. [Online]. Available:
https://www.transparentchoice.com/. [Accessed 5 February 2019].

[135] Wikipedia, "Thomas L. Saaty," 4 December 2018. [Online].
Available: https://en.wikipedia.org/wiki/Thomas_L._Saaty. [Accessed
4 February 2019].

[136] J. G. Dolan and I. Stephen, "Risk Communication Formats for Low
Probability Events: An Exploratory Study of Patient Preferences,"
BMC Medical Informatics and Decision Making, 10 April 2008.
[Online]. Available: https://bmcmedinformdecismak.biomedcentral.
com/articles/10.1186/1472-6947-8-14. [Accessed 4 February 2019].

[137] Wikipedia, "Grady Booch," 18 December 2018. [Online]. Available:
https://en.wikipedia.org/wiki/Grady_Booch. [Accessed 5 February
2019].

[138] A. Peters, "Ideo Says the Future of Design Is Circular," Fast
Company, 20 January 2017. [Online]. Available: https://www.
fastcompany.com/3067365/ideo-says-the-future-of-design-is-circular.
[Accessed 11 January 2019].

[139] The Circular Design Guide, 2017. [Online]. Available: https://www.
circulardesignguide.com/. [Accessed 11 January 2019].

[140] Patagonia, "Worn Wear," 2019. [Online]. Available: https://
wornwear.patagonia.com/repair-and-care#/Device/Patagonia_Zipper.
[Accessed 11 January 2019].

[141] Wikipedia, "Game Theory," 31 December 2018. [Online]. Available:
https://en.wikipedia.org/wiki/Game_theory. [Accessed 11 January
2019].

[142] R. D. Fisher, Winning the Hardware-Software Game: Using Game
Theory to Optimize the Pace of New Technology Adoption, 1 ed.,
Upper Saddle River, NJ: Prentice Hall, 2009, p. 272.

[143] R. Ladd, Personal Communication, 2019.

[144] L. Kemp, "Guest Post: A Knowledge Management System Capable of
Blinking Red," Quantellia, 26 August 2016. [Online]. Available:
https://www.lorienpratt.com/guest-post-a-knowledge-management-
system-capable-of-blinking-red/. [Accessed 11 January 2019].

[145] J. Mcgregor, "Gospels of Failure," Fast Company, 1 February 2005. [Online]. Available: https://www.fastcompany.com/52512/gospels-failure. [Accessed 11 January 2019].

[146] F. D. Flam, "The Odds, Continually Updated," The New York Times, 29 September 2014. [Online]. Available: http://mobile.nytimes.com/2014/09/30/science/the-odds-continually-updated.html. [Accessed 11 January 2019].

[147] J. Brewer, "Now Is the Time to Be Rooted in Reality," 14 July 2014. Available: https://upliftconnect.com/rooted-in-reality/

[148] J. Gots, "How World of Warcraft Could Save Your Business and the Economy," Big Think, 3 August 2012. [Online]. Available: https://bigthink.com/think-tank/how-world-of-warcraft-could-save-your-business-and-the-economy. [Accessed 31 January 2019]

[149] D. Smith, *Personal Communication*, 2019.

[150] Quantellia, "The Health Policy Simulation Tipping Point: A Decision Modeling Introduction," July 2012. [Online]. Available: https://www.youtube.com/watch?v=mGBUybAPuq4. [Accessed 31 January 2019].

[151] PWC, "The Art and Science of Big Decisions," February 2015. [Online]. Available: https://www.pwc.com/us/en/services/consulting/library/art-and-science-of-big-decisions.html. [Accessed 10 February 2019].

[152] J. Pearl and D. Mackenzie, *The Book of Why: The New Science of Cause and Effect*, New York, NY: Basic Books, 2018, p. 432. [Online]. Available: https://www.amazon.com/Book-Why-Science-Cause-Effect/dp/046509760X. [Accessed 11 January 2019].

[153] M. M. Ellamil, "Different Modes of Thought during the Creative Process," University of British Columbia, November 2010. Available: https://open.library.ubc.ca/cIRcle/collections/ubctheses/24/items/1.0071165

[154] J. R. Minkel, "Happiness: Good for Creativity, Bad for Single-minded Focus," *Scientific American Mind*, 2019. [Online]. Available: https://www.scientificamerican.com/article/happiness-good-for-creati/. [Accessed 31 January 2019].

[155] G. Rowe, J. B. Hirsh and A. K. Anderson, "Positive Affect Increases the Breadth of Attentional Selection,". Proceedings of the National Academy of Science of the United States of America, 2 January 2007 [Online]. Available: https://www.pnas.org/content/104/1/383.full. [Accessed 31 January 2019].

[156] G. Harrison, "Any Road," [Online]. Available: https://en.wikipedia. org/wiki/Any_Road.

[157] E. Brynjolfsson and A. McAfee, *The Second Machine Age: Work, Progress, and Prosperity in a Time of Brilliant Technologies*, New York, NY: W. W. Norton & Company, 2016, p. 121.

[158] L. Pratt, "Empathy: The Core of Complex Decisions," 29 August 2016. [Online]. Available: https://www.youtube.com/watch?v=VXZ-HDsIB-0. [Accessed 10 February 2019].

[159] L. Pratt, "Death by Proxy," 24 November 2016. [Online]. Available: https://www.lorienpratt.com/death-by-proxy/. [Accessed 11 January 2019].

[160] N. Ahmed, "How Collective Intelligence Can Change Your World, Right Now," 11 January 2019. [Online]. Available: https://medium. com/insurge-intelligence/how-collective-intelligence-can-change-your-world-right-now-fcfab215251f?fbclid=IwAR2SVqsU80SuExuwlfd 97iE5WgTn-LEm9kARF3oe6CXrfGHGRFe6cJEzccI. [Accessed 28 January 2019].

[161] A. Thakar, *Personal Communication*, 2019.

[162] Element Data, "Decision Intelligence at Your Fingertips," [Online]. Available: https://decisioncloud.io/platform/. [Accessed 11 February 2019].

[163] Quantellia, "Modeling Energy Strategies for the Cable Industry," 14 June 2013. Available: http://037cc9e.netsolhost.com/bl1/post/ 2013/06/14/Modeling-Energy-Strategies-for-the-Cable-Industry.aspx

[164] Quantellia/Bloomberg, "Getting Ahead of the Curve: Understanding Cable Energy Decisions," YouTube, 9 June 2013. [Online]. Available: https://www.youtube.com/watch?v=zaH5gohQQT0&feature=youtu. be. [Accessed 5 February 2019].

[165] "The Carter Center," February 2019. [Online]. Available: https://
www.cartercenter.org/. [Accessed 5 February 2019].

[166] Quantellia, "Modeling Economic Effects of Community Justice in
Liberia," [Online]. Available: http://corp.quantellia.com/liberia/
Liberiamodel.aspx. [Accessed 11 February 2019].

[167] Wikipedia, "Value Network Analysis," [Online]. Available: https://en.
wikipedia.org/wiki/Value_network_analysis.

[168] L. Pratt, "Beyond Data (Part 2): Big-O Snowballs, Copycats, and
Super Levers," 11 August 2015. [Online]. Available: https://www.
lorienpratt.com/beyond-data-part-2-big-o-snowballs-copycats-and-
super-levers/. [Accessed 5 February 2019].

[169] L. Pratt, "Responsibility, Authority, and Insanity," 22 November
2016. [Online]. Available: https://www.lorienpratt.com/responsibility-
authority-and-insanity/. [Accessed 5 February 2019].

[170] Wikipedia, "Moral Hazard," 30 November 2018. [Online].
Available: https://en.wikipedia.org/wiki/Moral_hazard. [Accessed
5 February 2019].

[171] Investopedia, "How Did Moral Hazard Contribute to the 2008
Financial Crisis?," 2017. Available: https://www.investopedia.com/
ask/answers/050515/how-did-moral-hazard-contribute-financial-
crisis-2008.asp

[172] Obama White House, "Fact Sheet: Data to Knowledge to Action:
Progress by Federal Agencies," 12 November 2013. [Online].
Available: https://obamawhitehouse.archives.gov/sites/default/files/
microsites/ostp/Data2Action%20Agency%20Progress.pdf. [Accessed
11 February 2019].

[173] O. Scharmer, "Capitalism 4.0 & Neuroplasticity of the Collective
Brain," HuffPost, 24 April 2014. [Online]. Available: https://www.
huffpost.com/entry/capitalism-40-and-neuropl_b_4839429

[174] D. Gabor, "We Cannot Predict the Future, But We Can Invent It,"
14 April 2016. [Online]. Available: https://quoteinvestigator.com/
2012/09/27/invent-the-future/. [Accessed 28 January 2019].

[175] L. Pratt, "Two Kinds of Software: It's Time to Take World Modeling Seriously," It's time to take world modeling seriously, 25 February 2015. [Online]. Available: https://www.lorienpratt.com/its-time-to-take-world-modeling-seriously/. [Accessed 29 January 2019].

[176] L. Pratt, "Leadership for Decision Makers," 2019. [Online]. Available: https://www.lorienpratt.com/category/leadership-decision-makers/. [Accessed 29 January 2019].

[177] J. Pritchard, "Moral Hazard: Definition and Examples: Taking Risks Without responsibility," The Balance, 23 February 2019. [Online]. Available: https://www.thebalance.com/moral-hazard-what-it-is-and-how-it-works-315515. [Accessed 11 March 2019].

[178] C. Kozyrkov, "The Simplest Explanation of Machine Learning You'll Ever Read," Hacker Noon, 24 May 2018. [Online]. Available: https://hackernoon.com/the-simplest-explanation-of-machine-learning-youll-ever-read-bebc0700047c. [Accessed 29 January 2019].

[179] D. Puckett, Director, N. Ahmed, *The Crisis of Civilization*. [Film]. YouTube, 2012. [Online]. Available: https://youtu.be/pMgOTQ7D_lk. [Accessed 8 March 2019].

[180] A. Nafeez, *Personal Communication*, 2019.

[181] N. Ahmed, "Insurge Intelligence," Patreon, 8 March 2019. [Online]. Available: https://www.patreon.com/nafeez.

[182] Office of the Director of National Intelligence (ODNI), "Vision 2015: A Globally Networked and Integrated Intelligence Enterprise," Washington, DC, 2008. [Online]. Available: http://www.ok-safe.com/files/documents/1/Vision_2015_Intelligence_Enterprise.pdf. [Accessed 9 February 2019].

[183] N. J. MacGaffin and P. C. Oleson, "Decision Advantage, Decision Confidence: The Why of Intelligence," *Intelligencer Journal, vol. 21*, no. 3, Fall/Winter, 2015.

[184] L. Pratt, "Senate Intelligence Briefing Features AI and Decision Advantage," Link, 13 February 2018. [Online]. Available: https://www.lorienpratt.com/senate-intelligence-briefing-features-ai-and-decision-advantage/. [Accessed 9 February 2019].

[185] F. Spencer, "How the Evolution of the Web Illustrates Our
       Transforming Relationship with Complexity and Connectivity,"
       2017. [Online]. Available: http://thefuturesschool.com/blog/hyperweb-
       how-the-evolution-of-the-web-is-transforming-our-relationship-to-
       complexity-and-connectivity/. [Accessed 5 February 2019].

[186] Wikipedia, "There's a Great Big Beautiful Tomorrow," 17 December
       2018. [Online]. Available: https://en.wikipedia.org/wiki/There%27s_
       a_Great_Big_Beautiful_Tomorrow. [Accessed 5 February 2019].

[187] W. Churchill, *Churchill By Himself: In His Own Words*,
       New York, NY: Rosetta Books, 2013.

[188] Wikipedia, "Total Quality Management," [Online]. Available: https://
       en.wikipedia.org/wiki/Total_quality_management. [Accessed 6 April
       2019].

[189] "Global Challenges Collaboration," [Online]. Available: https://
       globalchallengescollaboration.wordpress.com/. [Accessed 6 February
       2019].

[190] K. Schwab, *The Fourth Industrial Revolution*, Random House, 2017.
       [Online]. Available: https://www.amazon.com/dp/B01JEMROIU/ref=
       dp-kindle-redirect?_encoding=UTF8&btkr=1

[191] "About Long Now," The Long Now Foundation. [Online]. Available:
       http://longnow.org/about/. [Accessed 29 January 2019].

[192] N. Helmer, *Personal Communication*, March 2019.

[193] P. Manney, *Personal Communication,* (email), 2019.

[194] t. N. Hanh, "Awakening from the Illusion of Separation," Uplift,
       5 March 2016. [Online]. Available: https://upliftconnect.com/illusion-
       of-separation/. [Accessed 6 February 2019].

[195] K. C. Laslo, "From Systems Thinking to System Being," Magenta
       Wisdom, 9 August 2014. [Online]. Available: http://www.
       magentawisdom.net/systems-thinking–being/from-systems-thinking-
       to-systems-being. [Accessed 6 February 2019].

[196] J. Park, "Topic Quests: Knowing in the Wild," [Online]. Available:
       http://www.topicquests.org/. [Accessed 11 February 2019].

[197] Was Gandhi racist and casteist, 17 December 2016. [Online]. Available: https://www.theguardian.com/world/2016/oct/06/ghana-academics-petition-removal-mahatma-gandhi-statue-african-heroes

[198] Wikipedia, "Trusteeship," 11 February 2019. [Online]. Available: https://en.wikipedia.org/wiki/Trusteeship_(Gandhism).

[199] V. R. Ferose and L. Pratt, "Shifting at the Edge: Gandhi, AI, and Beyond," *Responsible AI/DI Ecosystem*, 30 August 2018. [Online]. Available: https://aidisummit.org/2018/08/30/shifting-at-the-edge-gandhi-ai-and-beyond/. [Accessed 11 February 2019].

[200] V. Ferose, *Personal Communication*, 2019.

[201] M. Lava, "Paradigm Shift," 15 July 2018. [Online]. Available: https://moultonlava.blogspot.com/2018/07/paradigm-shift.html?m=1. [Accessed 09 03 2019].

[202] F. Spencer, "Turning Wicked Problems into Wicked Opportunities," Fast Company, 5 May 2013. [Online]. Available: https://www.fastcompany.com/2682062/turning-wicked-problems-into-wicked-opportunities?fbclid=IwAR2xSMFVJkjkIZAcnxFjegBhg-3Xybnq5HngFHBue9TPabgKJ5ic6dxEhOk. [Accessed 9 February 2019].

[203] T. C. Boyle, *Without a Hero: And Other Stories*, New York, NY: Viking Press, 1994. [Online]. Available: http://www.amazon.com/gp/product/B000MRGW6W/ref=olp_product_details?ie=UTF8&me=&seller=. [Accessed 26 January 2019].

[204] Y. Bar-Yam, "Complexity Rising: From Human Beings to Human Civilization, a," in *Encyclopedia of Life Support Systems*, United Nations, Eolss Publishers, Paris, France, 2002. [Online]. Available: http://www.necsi.edu/projects/yaneer/EOLSSComplexityRising.pdf. [Accessed 26 January 2019].

[205] Google, "Trends over Time," Google Trends, 2019. [Online]. Available: https://trends.google.com/trends/explore?date=all&q=system%20dynamics,big%20data,artificial%20intelligence,machine%20learning,complex%20systems. [Accessed 11 January 2019].

[206] S. Ananda, "Small Data Requires Specialized Deep Learning and Yann LeCun Response," KDnuggets, March 2015. [Online]. Available: https://www.kdnuggets.com/2015/03/small-data-specialized-deep-learning-yann-lecun.html. [Accessed 11 January 2019].

[207] Wikipedia, "Quality Assurance," 13 December 2018. [Online]. Available: https://en.wikipedia.org/wiki/Quality_assurance. [Accessed 11 January 2019].

[208] Google, "Design Thinking Books," 2019. [Online]. Available: https://bit.ly/2Sk8FNU. [Accessed 11 January 2019].

[209] V. Ferose, "Differently-abled People Remind Us of the Value of Compassion," VR Ferose, 2019. [Online]. Available: https://ferosevr.com/differently-abled-people-remind-us-value-compassion/. [Accessed 11 January 2019].

[210] D. F. Wallace, "David Foster Wallace, in His Own Words," The Economist 1843, 19 September 2008. [Online]. Available: https://www.1843magazine.com/story/david-foster-wallace-in-his-own-words. [Accessed 11 January 2019].

[211] M. E. P. Seligman, P. Railton R. F. Baumeister and C. Sripada, "Navigating into the Future or Driven by the Past," *Perspectives on Psychological Science, vol. 8*, no. 2, pp. 119–141, 2013, Association for Psychological Science, Sage Journals. [Online]. Available: https://scottbarrykaufman.com/wp-content/uploads/2015/11/Perspectives-on-Psychological-Science-2013-Seligman-119-41.pdf

[212] Udacity, "Quiz – Intro to Machine Learning," YouTube, 23 February 2016. [Online]. Available: https://www.youtube.com/watch?v=TeFF9wXiFfs&feature=youtu.be. [Accessed 11 January 2019].

[213] L. Pratt, "Time for Big Data and Machine Learning to Take a Bold Step Forward...into 1946," 24 March 2015. [Online]. Available: http://www.lorienpratt.com/time-for-big-data-and-machine-learning-to-take-a-bold-step-forward-into-1946/. [Accessed 11 January 2019].

[214] R. Ladd, "How and Why I Got Here," Rick Ladd, 2014. [Online]. Available: https://rickladd.com/About-2/. [Accessed 11 January 2019].

[215] V. Granville, "Data Science Without Statistics Is Possible, Even Desirable," Data Science Without Statistics Is Possible, 8 December 2014. [Online]. Available: https://www.datasciencecentral.com/profiles/blogs/data-science-without-statistics-is-possible-even-desirable. [Accessed 11 January 2019].

[216] L. Pratt, "Decision Models Are the Requirements Language for DI Apps," 9 April 2015. [Online]. Available: https://www.lorienpratt.com/decision-models-are-the-requirements-language-for-di-apps/. [Accessed 11 January 2019].

[217] TDI3, "Web Presentation: The Business Case for Decision Intelligence," 17 October 2013. [Online]. Available: https://bit.ly/2SlyJYP. [Accessed 11 January 2019].

[218] J. Abidi, "Current Status of Employment of Disabled People in Indian Industries," *Asia Pacific Disability Rehabilitation Journal*, 1999. [Online]. Available: http://www.dinf.ne.jp/doc/english/asia/resource/apdrj/z13jo0400/z13jo0410.html.

[219] ILOSTAT Database, "Labor Force, Total," The World Bank, September 2018. [Online]. Available: https://data.worldbank.org/indicator/SL.TLF.TOTL.IN?end=2015&locations=IN&start=2014. [Accessed 11 January 2019].

[220] D. L. Pratt, "Optimized Decision Making (a Short History of the Future) – Webinar," YouTube, 27 February 2014. [Online]. Available: https://www.youtube.com/watch?v=79W1QKS1Pmw&feature=youtu.be. [Accessed 11 January 2019].

[221] "Telco 2.0," [Online]. Available: http://www.telco2.net/blog/. [Accessed 28 January 2019].

[222] J. Kerbel, "Lost for Words: The Intelligence Community's Struggle to Find its Voice," 2008. [Online]. Available: https://www.hsdl.org/?abstract&did=487668

[223] C. A. Medina, "What to Do When Traditional Models Fail," Studies in Intelligence, 2004. Available: https://www.cia.gov/library/center-for-the-study-of-intelligence/csi-publications/csi-studies/studies/vol46no3/article03.html

[224] National Academy of Clinical Biochemistry (NACB), "Laboratory Medicine Practice Guidelines: Evidence-based Practice for Point-of-care Testing," Washington, DC, 2006.

[225] T. Robbins, *Still Life with Woodpecker*, UK: Sidgwick & Jackson, 1980.

[226] Quantellia, "Breakthrough Machine Learning and Decision Intelligence," Quantellia, 2019. [Online]. Available: https://quantellia.com/. [Accessed 28 January 2019].

[227] "Walt Disney's original E.P.C.O.T film," 1966. © The Walt Disney Company. [Online]. Available: https://www.youtube.com/watch?reload=9&v=sLCHg9mUBag

[228] Quantellia, "Quantellia Technology Transformation with Cisco," Quantellia, 2017. [Online]. Available: https://quantellia.com/quantellia-technology-transformation-with-cisco-2/. [Accessed 5 February 2019].

[229] Wikipedia, "Conway's Game of Life," 24 January 2019. [Online]. Available: https://en.wikipedia.org/wiki/Conway%27s_Game_of_Life. [Accessed 5 February 2019].

[230] "Decision Intelligence Boosts Analytical Insight for New Network Designs and Business Monetization," Digital Journal, 26 March 2014. [Online]. Available: https://www.marketwatch.com/press-release/decision-intelligence-boosts-analytical-insight-for-new-network-designs-and-business-monetization-strategies-2014-03-26

[231] I. Emsley, J. Hartmann, L. Pratt, A. Colby and G. Panagos, "Navigating the telecom ship The CEM Control Center Catalyst," Quantellia, 2010. [Online]. Available: https://quantellia.com/Data/CEMControlCenterCatalystTMFNice2010b.pdf. [Accessed 5 February 2019].

[232] V. Barhat, "China Is Determined to Steal A.I. Crown from US and Nothing, Not Even a Trade War, Will Stop It," CNBC, 4 May 2018. [Online]. Available: https://www.cnbc.com/2018/05/04/china-aims-to-steal-us-a-i-crown-and-not-even-trade-war-will-stop-it.html. [Accessed 9 February 2019].

[233] LLC, Quantellia, "Modeling Economic Effects of Community Justice in Liberia," [Online]. Available: http://corp.quantellia.com/liberia/ Liberiamodel.aspx.

[234] E. R. Nesvold, A. Greenberg, N. Erasmus, E. van Heerden, J. L. Galache, E. Dahlstrom and F. Marchis, "The Deflector Selector: A Machine Learning Framework for Prioritizing Hazardous Object Deflection Technology Development," *Acta Astronautica, vol. 146,* 2018. [Online]. Available: https://arxiv.org/abs/1802.00458

[235] "FDL: Artificial Intelligence Research for Space Exploration and All Humankind," NASA. [Online]. Available: https://frontierdevelopmentlab. org/. [Accessed 11 February 2019].

[236] L. Pratt, CMU SV Guest Speaker Lorien Pratt, 16 April 2014, YouTube, Mountain View, CA, 2014. [Online]. Available: https:// www.youtube.com/watch?v=BzigRlLAjPE&feature=youtu.be&t=815. [Accessed 11 February 2019].

[237] J. Park, *Taming Conversation,* TEDx Temecula, 1 November 2018. [Online]. Available: https://www.youtube.com/watch?v=rtTSQ6B55fg

[238] V. Ferose and K. Raghavendra, "From Data to Model Risk: The Enterprise AI/DI Risk Management Challenge," *Digitalist Magazine,* 24 January 2019. [Online]. Available: https://www.digitalistmag.com/ cio-knowledge/2019/01/24/from-data-to-model-risk-enterprise-ai-di-risk-management-challenge-part-1-06195967. [Accessed 11 February 2019].

INDEX

Absolutdata, 4, 170
AGI. *See* Artificial General
        Intelligence (AGI)
Ahmed, Nafeez Masada, 136,
        163
AHP. *See* Analytic hierarchy
        process (AHP)
AI. *See* Artificial Intelligence (AI)
AIG, 4
Alibaba, 4
Amazon, 75
Analytic hierarchy process (AHP),
        101–102
Artificial General Intelligence
        (AGI), 3, 175
    robots, 2
Artificial Intelligence (AI), 2, 68,
        72–79
    in context, 78–79
    decision intelligence bridges
        from, 60–63
    DI as software engineering
        discipline for, 161
    ethics and responsibility,
        160–161
    expert systems, 77
    history: winters and summers,
        73–74
    market, 73
    natural language processing
        (NLP), 76
    reinforcement learning (RL)
        systems, 77
    supervised learning, 76–78

understanding the core of,
        74–76
unsupervised learning, 77
Asaro, Peter, 82
Asimov, Isaac, 63

Bateson, Gregory, 65, 79, 89
Bateson, Nora, 43, 70, 71, 72,
        170
Berry, Benjamin, 139
Big Data, 2, 67–70, 91
Blackman, Reid, 160–161
Bloomberg, 44
BPM. *See* Business process
        management (BPM)
Brant, Steve, 91, 183–184
Brewer, Joe, 88, 109
Brown, John Seely, 110
Brynjolfsson, Erik, 120
Busigence, 4, 170
Business process management
        (BPM), 112, 167
Business tracking discipline, DI as,
        164

Cable company sustainable
        energy generation,
        142–143
CAD. *See* Computer-assisted
        design (CAD)
Call detail records (CDRs), 150
Carter Center, 143
Casart, Jim, 19, 83, 164,
        183, 184